PORTFOLIO MANAGEMENT IN PRACTICE WORKBOOK

Volume 2

CFA Institute is the premier association for investment professionals around the world, with over 170,000 members more than 160 countries. Since 1963 the organization has developed and administered the renowned Chartered Financial Analyst Program. With a rich history of leading the investment profession, CFA Institute has set the highest standards in ethics, education, and professional excellence within the global investment community, and is the foremost authority on investment profession conduct and practice.

Each book in the CFA Institute Investment Series is geared toward industry practitioners along with graduate-level finance students and covers the most important topics in the industry. The authors of these cutting-edge books are themselves industry professionals and academics and bring their wealth of knowledge and expertise to this series.

PORTFOLIO MANAGEMENT IN PRACTICE WORKBOOK

Volume 2

Asset Allocation

WILEY

Cover image: © r.nagy/Shutterstock
Cover design: Wiley

Published by John Wiley & Sons, Inc., Hoboken, New Jersey.
Published simultaneously in Canada.

For general information on our other products and services or for technical support, please contact our Customer Care Department within the United States at (800) 762-2974, outside the United States at (317) 572-3993, or fax (317) 572-4002.

Wiley publishes in a variety of print and electronic formats and by print-on-demand. Some material included with standard print versions of this book may not be included in e-books or in print-on-demand. If this book refers to media such as a CD or DVD that is not included in the version you purchased, you may download this material at http://booksupport.wiley.com. For more information about Wiley products, visit www.wiley.com.

ISBN 978-1-119-78808-9
ISBN 978-1-119-78824-9 (ePDF)
ISBN 978-1-119-78816-4 (ePub)

Printed in the United States of America.
SKY10022154_110220

CONTENTS

Contents

PART I

LEARNING OBJECTIVES, SUMMARY OVERVIEW, AND PROBLEMS

CHAPTER 1

BASICS OF PORTFOLIO PLANNING AND CONSTRUCTION

LEARNING OUTCOMES

The candidate should be able to:

- describe the reasons for a written investment policy statement (IPS);
- describe the major components of an IPS;
- describe risk and return objectives and how they may be developed for a client;
- distinguish between the willingness and the ability (capacity) to take risk in analyzing an investor's financial risk tolerance;
- describe the investment constraints of liquidity, time horizon, tax concerns, legal and regulatory factors, and unique circumstances and their implications for the choice of portfolio assets;
- explain the specification of asset classes in relation to asset allocation;
- describe the principles of portfolio construction and the role of asset allocation in relation to the IPS;
- describe how environmental, social, and governance (ESG) considerations may be integrated into portfolio planning and construction.

SUMMARY

In this chapter, we have discussed construction of a client's investment policy statement, including discussion of risk and return objectives and the various constraints that will apply to the portfolio. We have also discussed the portfolio construction process, with emphasis on the strategic asset allocation decisions that must be made.

- The IPS is the starting point of the portfolio management process. Without a full understanding of the client's situation and requirements, it is unlikely that successful results will be achieved.
- The IPS can take a variety of forms. A typical format will include the client's investment objectives and also list the constraints that apply to the client's portfolio.
- The client's objectives are specified in terms of risk tolerance and return requirements.
- The constraints section covers factors that need to be considered when constructing a portfolio for the client that meets the objectives. The typical constraint categories are liquidity requirements, time horizon, regulatory requirements, tax status, and unique needs.
- Clients may have personal objections to certain products or practices, which could lead to the exclusion of certain companies, countries, or types of securities from the investable universe as well as the client's benchmark. Such considerations are often referred to as ESG (environmental, social, governance).
- ESG considerations can be integrated into an investment policy by exclusionary screening, best-in-class selection, active ownership, thematic and impact investing, and ESG integration in security analysis.
- Risk objectives are specifications for portfolio risk that reflect the risk tolerance of the client. Quantitative risk objectives can be absolute or relative or a combination of the two.
- The client's overall risk tolerance is a function of the client's ability to accept risk and their "risk attitude," which can be considered the client's willingness to take risk.
- The client's return objectives can be stated on an absolute or a relative basis. As an example of an absolute objective, the client may want to achieve a particular percentage rate of return. Alternatively, the return objective can be stated on a relative basis, for example, relative to a benchmark return.
- The liquidity section of the IPS should state what the client's requirements are to draw cash from the portfolio.
- The time horizon section of the IPS should state the time horizon over which the investor is investing. This horizon may be the period during which the portfolio is accumulating before any assets need to be withdrawn.
- Tax status varies among investors and a client's tax status should be stated in the IPS.
- The IPS should state any legal or regulatory restrictions that constrain the investment of the portfolio.
- The unique circumstances section of the IPS should cover any other aspect of a client's circumstances that is likely to have a material impact on the composition of the portfolio. Certain ESG implementation approaches, such as negative (exclusionary) screening, best-in-class, thematic investing, impact investing, and ESG integration may be discussed in this section.
- Asset classes are the building blocks of an asset allocation. An asset class is a category of assets that have similar characteristics, attributes, and risk/return relationships. Traditionally, investors have distinguished cash, equities, bonds, and real estate as the major asset classes.
- A strategic asset allocation results from combining the constraints and objectives articulated in the IPS and capital market expectations regarding the asset classes.
- As time goes on, a client's asset allocation will drift from the target allocation, and the amount of allowable drift as well as a rebalancing policy should be formalized.

- In addition to taking systematic risk, an investment committee may choose to take tactical asset allocation risk or security selection risk. The amount of return attributable to these decisions can be measured.
- ESG considerations may be integrated into the portfolio planning and construction process. Such considerations can be difficult given that ESG data is often not required to be disclosed by companies. ESG implementation approaches require a set of instructions for investment managers with regards to the selection of securities, the exercise of shareholder rights, and the selection of investment strategies.

PRACTICE PROBLEMS

1. Which of the following is *least important* as a reason for a written investment policy statement (IPS)?
   A. The IPS may be required by regulation.
   B. Having a written IPS is part of best practice for a portfolio manager.
   C. Having a written IPS ensures the client's risk and return objectives can be achieved.

2. Which of the following *best* describes the underlying rationale for a written investment policy statement (IPS)?
   A. A written IPS communicates a plan for trying to achieve investment success.
   B. A written IPS provides investment managers with a ready defense against client lawsuits.
   C. A written IPS allows investment managers to instruct clients about the proper use and purpose of investments.

3. A written investment policy statement (IPS) is *most likely* to succeed if:
   A. it is created by a software program to assure consistent quality.
   B. it is a collaborative effort of the client and the portfolio manager.
   C. it reflects the investment philosophy of the portfolio manager.

4. The section of the investment policy statement (IPS) that provides information about how policy may be executed, including restrictions and exclusions, is *best* described as the:
   A. *Investment Objectives.*
   B. *Investment Guidelines.*
   C. *Statement of Duties and Responsibilities.*

5. Which of the following is *least likely* to be placed in the appendices to an investment policy statement (IPS)?
   A. *Rebalancing Policy*
   B. *Strategic Asset Allocation*
   C. *Statement of Duties and Responsibilities*

6. Which of the following typical topics in an investment policy statement (IPS) is *most closely* linked to the client's "distinctive needs"?
   A. *Procedures*
   B. *Investment Guidelines*
   C. *Statement of Duties and Responsibilities*

7. An investment policy statement that includes a return objective of outperforming the FTSE 100 by 120 basis points is *best* characterized as having a(n):
   A. relative return objective.
   B. absolute return objective.
   C. arbitrage-based return objective.

8. Risk assessment questionnaires for investment management clients are *most* useful in measuring:
   A. value at risk.
   B. ability to take risk.
   C. willingness to take risk.

9. Which of the following is *best* characterized as a relative risk objective?
   A. Value at risk for the fund will not exceed US$3 million.
   B. The fund will not underperform the DAX by more than 250 basis points.
   C. The fund will not lose more than €2.5 million in the coming 12-month period.

10. In preparing an investment policy statement, which of the following is *most difficult* to quantify?
    A. Time horizon
    B. Ability to accept risk
    C. Willingness to accept risk

11. After interviewing a client in order to prepare a written investment policy statement (IPS), you have established the following:
    - The client has earnings that vary dramatically between £30,000 and £70,000 (pre-tax) depending on weather patterns in Britain.
    - In three of the previous five years, the after-tax income of the client has been less than £20,000.
    - The client's mother is dependent on her son (the client) for approximately £9,000 per year support.
    - The client's own subsistence needs are approximately £12,000 per year.
    - The client has more than 10 years' experience trading investments including commodity futures, stock options, and selling stock short.
    - The client's responses to a standard risk assessment questionnaire suggest he has above average risk tolerance.

    The client is *best* described as having a:
    A. low ability to take risk, but a high willingness to take risk.
    B. high ability to take risk, but a low willingness to take risk.
    C. high ability to take risk and a high willingness to take risk.

12. After interviewing a client in order to prepare a written investment policy statement (IPS), you have established the following:
    - The client has earnings that have exceeded €120,000 (pre-tax) each year for the past five years.
    - She has no dependents.
    - The client's subsistence needs are approximately €45,000 per year.
    - The client states that she feels uncomfortable with her lack of understanding of securities markets.

- All of the client's current savings are invested in short-term securities guaranteed by an agency of her national government.
- The client's responses to a standard risk assessment questionnaire suggest she has low risk tolerance.

The client is *best* described as having a:
A. low ability to take risk, but a high willingness to take risk.
B. high ability to take risk, but a low willingness to take risk.
C. high ability to take risk and a high willingness to take risk.

13. A client who is a 34-year-old widow with two healthy young children (aged 5 and 7) has asked you to help her form an investment policy statement. She has been employed as an administrative assistant in a bureau of her national government for the previous 12 years. She has two primary financial goals—her retirement and providing for the college education of her children. This client's time horizon is *best* described as being:
A. long term.
B. short term.
C. medium term.

14. The timing of payouts for property and casualty insurers is unpredictable ("lumpy") in comparison with the timing of payouts for life insurance companies. Therefore, in general, property and casualty insurers have:
A. lower liquidity needs than life insurance companies.
B. greater liquidity needs than life insurance companies.
C. a higher return objective than life insurance companies.

15. A client who is a director of a publicly listed corporation is required by law to refrain from trading that company's stock at certain points of the year when disclosure of financial results are pending. In preparing a written investment policy statement (IPS) for this client, this restriction on trading:
A. is irrelevant to the IPS.
B. should be included in the IPS.
C. makes it illegal for the portfolio manager to work with this client.

16. Consider the pairwise correlations of monthly returns of the following asset classes:

	Brazilian Equities	East Asian Equities	European Equities	US Equities
Brazilian equities	1.00	0.70	0.85	0.76
East Asian equities	0.70	1.00	0.91	0.88
European equities	0.85	0.91	1.00	0.90
US equities	0.76	0.88	0.90	1.00

Based solely on the information in the above table, which equity asset class is *most sharply* distinguished from US equities?
A. Brazilian equities.
B. European equities.
C. East Asian equities.

17. Returns on asset classes are *best* described as being a function of:
    A. the failure of arbitrage.
    B. exposure to the idiosyncratic risks of those asset classes.
    C. exposure to sets of systematic factors relevant to those asset classes.

18. In defining asset classes as part of the strategic asset allocation decision, pairwise correlations within asset classes should generally be:
    A. equal to correlations among asset classes.
    B. lower than correlations among asset classes.
    C. higher than correlations among asset classes.

19. Tactical asset allocation is *best* described as:
    A. attempts to exploit arbitrage possibilities among asset classes.
    B. the decision to deliberately deviate from the policy portfolio.
    C. selecting asset classes with the desired exposures to sources of systematic risk in an investment portfolio.

CHAPTER 2

SECURITY MARKET INDEXES

LEARNING OUTCOMES

The candidate should be able to:

- describe a security market index;
- calculate and interpret the value, price return, and total return of an index;
- describe the choices and issues in index construction and management;
- compare the different weighting methods used in index construction;
- calculate and analyze the value and return of an index given its weighting method;
- describe rebalancing and reconstitution of an index;
- describe uses of security market indexes;
- describe types of equity indexes;
- describe types of fixed-income indexes;
- describe indexes representing alternative investments;
- compare types of security market indexes.

SUMMARY

This chapter explains and illustrates the construction, management, and uses of security market indexes. It also discusses various types of indexes. Security market indexes are invaluable tools for investors, who can select from among thousands of indexes representing a variety of security markets, market segments, and asset classes. These indexes range from those representing the global market for major asset classes to those representing alternative investments in specific geographic markets. To benefit from the use of security market indexes, investors must understand their construction and determine whether the selected index is appropriate for their purposes. Frequently, an index that is well suited for one purpose may not be well suited for other purposes. Users of indexes must be familiar with how various indexes are constructed in order to select the index or indexes most appropriate for their needs.

Among the key points made in this chapter are the following:

- Security market indexes are intended to measure the values of different target markets (security markets, market segments, or asset classes).
- The constituent securities selected for inclusion in the security market index are intended to represent the target market.
- A price return index reflects only the prices of the constituent securities.
- A total return index reflects not only the prices of the constituent securities but also the reinvestment of all income received since the inception of the index.
- Methods used to weight the constituents of an index range from the very simple, such as price and equal weightings, to the more complex, such as market-capitalization and fundamental weightings.
- Choices in index construction—in particular, the choice of weighting method—affect index valuation and returns.
- Index management includes 1) periodic rebalancing to ensure that the index maintains appropriate weightings and 2) reconstitution to ensure the index represents the desired target market.
- Rebalancing and reconstitution create turnover in an index. Reconstitution can dramatically affect prices of current and prospective constituents.
- Indexes serve a variety of purposes. They gauge market sentiment and serve as benchmarks for actively managed portfolios. They act as proxies for measuring systematic risk and risk-adjusted performance. They also serve as proxies for asset classes in asset allocation models and as model portfolios for investment products.
- Investors can choose from security market indexes representing various asset classes, including equity, fixed-income, commodity, real estate, and hedge fund indexes.
- Within most asset classes, index providers offer a wide variety of indexes, ranging from broad market indexes to highly specialized indexes based on the issuer's geographic region, economic development group, or economic sector or other factors.
- Proper use of security market indexes depends on understanding their construction and management.

PRACTICE PROBLEMS

1. A security market index represents the:
   A. risk of a security market.
   B. security market as a whole.
   C. security market, market segment, or asset class.

2. Security market indexes are:
   A. constructed and managed like a portfolio of securities.
   B. simple interchangeable tools for measuring the returns of different asset classes.
   C. valued on a regular basis using the actual market prices of the constituent securities.

3. When creating a security market index, an index provider must first determine the:
   A. target market.
   B. appropriate weighting method.
   C. number of constituent securities.

4. One month after inception, the price return version and total return version of a single index (consisting of identical securities and weights) will be equal if:
   A. market prices have not changed.
   B. capital gains are offset by capital losses.
   C. the securities do not pay dividends or interest.

5. The values of a price return index and a total return index consisting of identical equal-weighted dividend-paying equities will be equal:
   A. only at inception.
   B. at inception and on rebalancing dates.
   C. at inception and on reconstitution dates.

6. An analyst gathers the following information for an equal-weighted index comprised of assets Able, Baker, and Charlie:

Security	Beginning of Period Price (€)	End of Period Price (€)	Total Dividends (€)
Able	10.00	12.00	0.75
Baker	20.00	19.00	1.00
Charlie	30.00	30.00	2.00

The price return of the index is:
   A. 1.7%.
   B. 5.0%.
   C. 11.4%.

7. An analyst gathers the following information for an equal-weighted index comprised of assets Able, Baker, and Charlie:

Security	Beginning of Period Price (€)	End of Period Price (€)	Total Dividends (€)
Able	10.00	12.00	0.75
Baker	20.00	19.00	1.00
Charlie	30.00	30.00	2.00

The total return of the index is:
   A. 5.0%.
   B. 7.9%.
   C. 11.4%.

8. An analyst gathers the following information for a price-weighted index comprised of securities ABC, DEF, and GHI:

Security	Beginning of Period Price (£)	End of Period Price (£)	Total Dividends (£)
ABC	25.00	27.00	1.00
DEF	35.00	25.00	1.50
GHI	15.00	16.00	1.00

The price return of the index is:
A. −4.6%.
B. −9.3%.
C. −13.9%.

9. An analyst gathers the following information for a market-capitalization-weighted index comprised of securities MNO, QRS, and XYZ:

Security	Beginning of Period Price (¥)	End of Period Price (¥)	Dividends per Share (¥)	Shares Outstanding
MNO	2,500	2,700	100	5,000
QRS	3,500	2,500	150	7,500
XYZ	1,500	1,600	100	10,000

The price return of the index is:
A. −9.33%.
B. −10.23%.
C. −13.90%.

10. An analyst gathers the following information for a market-capitalization-weighted index comprised of securities MNO, QRS, and XYZ:

Security	Beginning of Period Price (¥)	End of Period Price (¥)	Dividends Per Share (¥)	Shares Outstanding
MNO	2,500	2,700	100	5,000
QRS	3,500	2,500	150	7,500
XYZ	1,500	1,600	100	10,000

The total return of the index is:
A. 1.04%.
B. −5.35%.
C. −10.23%.

11. When creating a security market index, the target market:
A. determines the investment universe.
B. is usually a broadly defined asset class.
C. determines the number of securities to be included in the index.

12. An analyst gathers the following data for a price-weighted index:

Security	Beginning of Period Price (€)	Beginning of Period Shares Outstanding	End of Period Price (€)	End of Period Shares Outstanding
A	20.00	300	22.00	300
B	50.00	300	48.00	300
C	26.00	2,000	30.00	2,000

The price return of the index over the period is:
A. 4.2%.
B. 7.1%.
C. 21.4%.

13. An analyst gathers the following data for a value-weighted index:

Security	Beginning of Period Price (£)	Beginning of Period Shares Outstanding	End of Period Price (£)	End of Period Shares Outstanding
A	20.00	300	22.00	300
B	50.00	300	48.00	300
C	26.00	2,000	30.00	2,000

The return on the value-weighted index over the period is:
A. 7.1%.
B. 11.0%.
C. 21.4%.

14. An analyst gathers the following data for an equally-weighted index:

Security	Beginning of Period Price (¥)	Beginning of Period Shares Outstanding	End of Period Price (¥)	End of Period Shares Outstanding
A	20.00	300	22.00	300
B	50.00	300	48.00	300
C	26.00	2,000	30.00	2,000

The return on the index over the period is:
A. 4.2%.
B. 6.8%.
C. 7.1%.

15. Which of the following index weighting methods requires an adjustment to the divisor after a stock split?
    A. Price weighting
    B. Fundamental weighting
    C. Market-capitalization weighting

16. If the price return of an equal-weighted index exceeds that of a market-capitalization-weighted index comprised of the same securities, the *most likely* explanation is:
    A. stock splits.
    B. dividend distributions.
    C. outperformance of small-market-capitalization stocks.

17. A float-adjusted market-capitalization-weighted index weights each of its constituent securities by its price and:
    A. its trading volume.
    B. the number of its shares outstanding.
    C. the number of its shares available to the investing public.

18. Which of the following index weighting methods is *most likely* subject to a value tilt?
    A. Equal weighting
    B. Fundamental weighting
    C. Market-capitalization weighting

19. Rebalancing an index is the process of periodically adjusting the constituent:
    A. securities' weights to optimize investment performance.
    B. securities to maintain consistency with the target market.
    C. securities' weights to maintain consistency with the index's weighting method.

20. Which of the following index weighting methods requires the *most frequent* rebalancing?
    A. Price weighting
    B. Equal weighting
    C. Market-capitalization weighting

21. Reconstitution of a security market index reduces:
    A. portfolio turnover.
    B. the need for rebalancing.
    C. the likelihood that the index includes securities that are not representative of the target market.

22. Security market indexes are used as:
    A. measures of investment returns.
    B. proxies to measure unsystematic risk.
    C. proxies for specific asset classes in asset allocation models.

23. Uses of market indexes do not include serving as a:
    A. measure of systemic risk.
    B. basis for new investment products.
    C. benchmark for evaluating portfolio performance.

24. Which of the following statements regarding sector indexes is *most accurate*? Sector indexes:
    A. track different economic sectors and cannot be aggregated to represent the equivalent of a broad market index.
    B. provide a means to determine whether an active investment manager is more successful at stock selection or sector allocation.
    C. apply a universally agreed upon sector classification system to identify the constituent securities of specific economic sectors, such as consumer goods, energy, finance, health care.

25. Which of the following is an example of a style index? An index based on:
    A. geography.
    B. economic sector.
    C. market capitalization.

26. Which of the following statements regarding fixed-income indexes is *most accurate*?
    A. Liquidity issues make it difficult for investors to easily replicate fixed-income indexes.
    B. Rebalancing and reconstitution are the only sources of turnover in fixed-income indexes.
    C. Fixed-income indexes representing the same target market hold similar numbers of bonds.

27. An aggregate fixed-income index:
    A. comprises corporate and asset-backed securities.
    B. represents the market of government-issued securities.
    C. can be subdivided by market or economic sector to create more narrowly defined indexes.

28. Fixed-income indexes are *least likely* constructed on the basis of:
    A. maturity.
    B. type of issuer.
    C. coupon frequency.

29. Commodity index values are based on:
    A. futures contract prices.
    B. the market price of the specific commodity.
    C. the average market price of a basket of similar commodities.

30. Which of the following statements is *most accurate*?
    A. Commodity indexes all share similar weighting methods.
    B. Commodity indexes containing the same underlying commodities offer similar returns.
    C. The performance of commodity indexes can be quite different from that of the underlying commodities.

31. Which of the following is *not* a real estate index category?
    A. Appraisal index
    B. Initial sales index
    C. Repeat sales index

32. A unique feature of hedge fund indexes is that they:
    A. are frequently equal weighted.
    B. are determined by the constituents of the index.
    C. reflect the value of private rather than public investments.

33. The returns of hedge fund indexes are *most likely*:
    A. biased upward.
    B. biased downward.
    C. similar across different index providers.

34. In comparison to equity indexes, the constituent securities of fixed-income indexes are:
    A. more liquid.
    B. easier to price.
    C. drawn from a larger investment universe.

CHAPTER 3

CAPITAL MARKET EXPECTATIONS, PART 1: FRAMEWORK AND MACRO CONSIDERATIONS

LEARNING OUTCOMES

The candidate should be able to:

- discuss the role of, and a framework for, capital market expectations in the portfolio management process;
- discuss challenges in developing capital market forecasts;
- explain how exogenous shocks may affect economic growth trends;
- discuss the application of economic growth trend analysis to the formulation of capital market expectations;
- compare major approaches to economic forecasting;
- discuss how business cycles affect short- and long-term expectations;
- explain the relationship of inflation to the business cycle and the implications of inflation for cash, bonds, equity, and real estate returns;
- discuss the effects of monetary and fiscal policy on business cycles;
- interpret the shape of the yield curve as an economic predictor and discuss the relationship between the yield curve and fiscal and monetary policy;
- identify and interpret macroeconomic, interest rate, and exchange rate linkages between economies.

SUMMARY

This is the first of two chapters on how investment professionals should address the setting of capital market expectations. The chapter began with a general framework for developing capital market expectations followed by a review of various challenges and pitfalls that analysts may encounter in the forecasting process. The remainder of the chapter focused on the use of macroeconomic analysis in setting expectations. The following are the main points covered in the chapter:

- Capital market expectations are essential inputs for strategic as well as tactical asset allocation.
- The ultimate objective is a set of projections with which to make informed investment decisions, specifically asset allocation decisions.
- Undue emphasis should not be placed on the accuracy of projections for individual asset classes. Internal consistency across asset classes (cross-sectional consistency) and over various time horizons (intertemporal consistency) are far more important objectives.
- The process of capital market expectations setting involves the following steps:
  1. Specify the set of expectations that are needed, including the time horizon(s) to which they apply.
  2. Research the historical record.
  3. Specify the method(s) and/or model(s) that will be used and their information requirements.
  4. Determine the best sources for information needs.
  5. Interpret the current investment environment using the selected data and methods, applying experience and judgment.
  6. Provide the set of expectations and document the conclusions.
  7. Monitor outcomes, compare to forecasts, and provide feedback.

- Among the challenges in setting capital market expectations are:
  - *limitations of economic data* including lack of timeliness as well as changing definitions and calculations;
  - *data measurement errors and biases* including transcription errors, survivorship bias, and appraisal (smoothed) data;
  - *limitations of historical estimates* including lack of precision, nonstationarity, asynchronous observations, and distributional considerations such as fat tails and skewness;
  - ex post *risk as a biased risk measure* such as when historical returns reflect expectations of a low-probability catastrophe that did not occur or capture a low-probability event that did happen to occur;
  - *bias in methods* including data-mining and time-period biases;
  - *failure to account for conditioning information*;
  - *misinterpretation of correlations*;
  - *psychological biases* including anchoring, status quo, confirmation, overconfidence, prudence, and availability biases.
  - *model uncertainty*.

- Losing sight of the connection between investment outcomes and the economy is a fundamental, and potentially costly, mistake in setting capital market expectations.

- Some growth trend changes are driven by slowly evolving and easily observable factors that are easy to forecast. Trend changes arising from exogenous shocks are impossible to forecast and difficult to identify, assess, and quantify until the change is well established.
- Among the most important sources of shocks are policy changes, new products and technologies, geopolitics, natural disasters, natural resources/critical inputs, and financial crises.
- An economy's aggregate trend growth rate reflects growth in labor inputs and growth in labor productivity. Extrapolating past trends in these components can provide a reasonable initial estimate of the future growth trend, which can be adjusted based on observable information. Less developed economies may require more significant adjustments because they are likely to be undergoing more rapid structural changes.
- The average level of real (nominal) default-free bond yields is linked to the trend rate of real (nominal) growth. The trend rate of growth provides an important anchor for estimating bond returns over horizons long enough for this reversion to prevail over cyclical and short-term forces.
- The trend growth rate provides an anchor for long-run equity appreciation. In the very long run, the aggregate value of equity must grow at a rate very close to the rate of GDP growth.
- There are three main approaches to economic forecasting:
  - *Econometric models*: structural and reduced-form statistical models of key variables generate quantitative estimates, impose discipline on forecasts, may be robust enough to approximate reality, and can readily forecast the impact of exogenous variables or shocks. However, they tend to be complex, time-consuming to formulate, and potentially mis-specified, and they rarely forecast turning points well.
  - *Indicators*: variables that lead, lag, or coincide with turns in the economy. This approach is the simplest, requiring only a limited number of published statistics. It can generate false signals, however, and is vulnerable to revisions that may overfit past data at the expense of the reliability of out-of-sample forecasts.
  - *Checklist(s)*: subjective integration of information deemed relevant by the analyst. This approach is the most flexible but also the most subjective. It readily adapts to a changing environment, but ongoing collection and assessment of information make it time-consuming and also limit the depth and consistency of the analysis.
- The business cycle is the result of many intermediate frequency cycles that jointly generate most of the variation in aggregate economic activity. This explains why historical business cycles have varied in both duration and intensity and why it is difficult to project turning points in real time.
- The business cycle reflects decisions that (a) are made based on imperfect information and/or analysis with the expectation of future benefits, (b) require significant current resources and/or time to implement, and (c) are difficult and/or costly to reverse. Such decisions are, broadly defined, investment decisions.
- A typical business cycle has a number of phases. We split the cycle into five phases with the following capital market implications:
  - **Initial Recovery.** Short-term interest rates and bond yields are low. Bond yields are likely to bottom. Stock markets may rise strongly. Cyclical/riskier assets such as small stocks, high-yield bonds, and emerging market securities perform well.
  - **Early Expansion.** Short rates are moving up. Longer-maturity bond yields are stable or rising slightly. Stocks are trending up.

- **Late Expansion.** Interest rates rise, and the yield curve flattens. Stock markets often rise but may be volatile. Cyclical assets may underperform while inflation hedges outperform.
- **Slowdown.** Short-term interest rates are at or nearing a peak. Government bond yields peak and may then decline sharply. The yield curve may invert. Credit spreads widen, especially for weaker credits. Stocks may fall. Interest-sensitive stocks and "quality" stocks with stable earnings perform best.
- **Contraction.** Interest rates and bond yields drop. The yield curve steepens. The stock market drops initially but usually starts to rise well before the recovery emerges. Credit spreads widen and remain elevated until clear signs of a cycle trough emerge.

- At least three factors complicate translation of business cycle information into capital market expectations and profitable investment decisions. First, the phases of the cycle vary in length and amplitude. Second, it is not always easy to distinguish between cyclical forces and secular forces acting on the economy and the markets. Third, how, when, and by how much the markets respond to the business cycle is as uncertain as the cycle itself—perhaps more so.
- Business cycle information is likely to be most reliable/valuable in setting capital market expectations over horizons within the range of likely expansion and contraction phases. Transitory developments cloud shorter-term forecasts, whereas significantly longer horizons likely cover portions of multiple cycle phases. Information about the current cyclical state of the economy has no predictive value over very long horizons.
- Monetary policy is often used as a mechanism for intervention in the business cycle. This mechanism is inherent in the mandates of most central banks to maintain price stability and/or growth consistent with potential.
- Monetary policy aims to be countercyclical, but the ability to fine-tune the economy is limited and policy measures may exacerbate rather than moderate the business cycle. This risk is greatest at the top of the cycle when the central bank may overestimate the economy's momentum and/or underestimate the potency of restrictive policies.
- Fiscal policy—government spending and taxation—can be used to counteract cyclical fluctuations in the economy. Aside from extreme situations, however, fiscal policy typically addresses objectives other than regulating short-term growth. So-called automatic stabilizers do play an important role in mitigating cyclical fluctuations.
- The Taylor rule is a useful tool for assessing a central bank's stance and for predicting how that stance is likely to evolve.
- The expectation that central banks could not implement negative policy rates proved to be unfounded in the aftermath of the 2007–2009 global financial crisis. Because major central banks combined negative policy rates with other extraordinary measures (notably quantitative easing), however, the effectiveness of the negative rate policy is unclear. The effectiveness of quantitative easing is also unclear.
- Negative interest rates, and the environment that gives rise to them, make the task of setting capital market expectations even more complex. Among the issues that arise are the following:
  - It is difficult to justify negative rates as a "risk-free rate" to which risk premiums can be added to establish long-term "equilibrium" asset class returns.
  - Historical data and quantitative models are even less likely to be reliable.
  - Market relationships (e.g., the yield curve) are likely to be distorted by other concurrent policy measures.

- The mix of monetary and fiscal policies has its most apparent effect on the average level of interest rates and inflation. Persistently loose (tight) fiscal policy increases (reduces) the average level of real interest rates. Persistently loose (tight) monetary policy increases (reduces) the average levels of actual and expected inflation. The impact on nominal rates is ambiguous if one policy is persistently tight and the other persistently loose.
- Changes in the slope of the yield curve are driven primarily by the evolution of short rate expectations, which are driven mainly by the business cycle and policies. The slope of the curve may also be affected by debt management.
- The slope of the yield curve is useful as a predictor of economic growth and as an indicator of where the economy is in the business cycle.
- Macroeconomic linkages between countries are expressed through their respective current and capital accounts.
- There are four primary mechanisms by which the current and capital accounts are kept in balance: changes in income (GDP), relative prices, interest rates and asset prices, and exchange rates.
- In the short run, interest rates, exchange rates, and financial asset prices must adjust to keep the capital account in balance with the more slowly evolving current account. The current account, in conjunction with real output and the relative prices of goods and services, tends to reflect secular trends and the pace of the business cycle.
- Interest rates and currency exchange rates are inextricably linked. This relationship is evident in the fact that a country cannot simultaneously allow unfettered capital flows, maintain a fixed exchange rate, and pursue an independent monetary policy.
- Two countries will share a default-free yield curve if (and only if) there is perfect capital mobility and the exchange rate is credibility fixed *forever*. It is the lack of credibly fixed exchange rates that allows (default-free) yield curves, and hence bond returns, to be less than perfectly correlated across markets.
- With floating exchange rates, the link between interest rates and exchange rates is primarily expectational. To equalize risk-adjusted expected returns across markets, interest rates must be higher (lower) in a currency that is expected to depreciate (appreciate). This dynamic can lead to the exchange rate "overshooting" in one direction to generate the expectation of movement in the opposite direction.
- An investor cares about the real return that he or she expects to earn *in his or her own currency*. In terms of a foreign asset, what matters is the *nominal* return and the change in the exchange rate.
- Although real interest rates around the world need not be equal, they are linked through the requirement that global savings must always equal global investment. Hence, they will tend to move together.

PRACTICE PROBLEMS

The following information relates to Questions 1–8

Neshie Wakuluk is an investment strategist who develops capital market expectations for an investment firm that invests across asset classes and global markets. Wakuluk started her career when the global markets were experiencing significant volatility and poor returns; as a result, she is now careful to base her conclusions on objective evidence and analytical procedures to mitigate any potential biases.

Wakuluk's approach to economic forecasting utilizes a structural model in conjunction with a diffusion index to determine the current phase of a country's business cycle. This approach has produced successful predictions in the past, thus Wakuluk has high confidence in the predictions. Wakuluk also determines whether any adjustments need to be made to her initial estimates of the respective aggregate economic growth trends based on historical rates of growth for Countries X and Y (both developed markets) and Country Z (a developing market). Exhibit 1 summarizes Wakuluk's predictions:

EXHIBIT 1   Prediction for Current Phase of the Business Cycle

Country X	Country Y	Country Z
Initial Recovery	Contraction	Late Upswing

Wakuluk assumes short-term interest rates adjust with expected inflation and are procyclical. Wakuluk reviews the historical short-term interest rate trends for each country, which further confirms her predictions shown in Exhibit 1.

Wakuluk decides to focus on Country Y to determine the path of nominal interest rates, the potential economic response of Country Y's economy to this path, and the timing for when Country Y's economy may move into the next business cycle. Wakuluk makes the following observations:

Observation 1:   Monetary policy has been persistently loose for Country Y, while fiscal policies have been persistently tight.

Observation 2:   Country Y is expected to significantly increase transfer payments and introduce a more progressive tax regime.

Observation 3:   The current yield curve for Country Y suggests that the business cycle is in the slowdown phase, with bond yields starting to reflect contractionary conditions.

1. Wakuluk *most likely* seeks to mitigate which of the following biases in developing capital market forecasts?
   A. Availability
   B. Time period
   C. Survivorship

2. Wakuluk's approach to economic forecasting:
   A. is flexible and limited in complexity.
   B. can give a false sense of precision and provide false signals.
   C. imposes no consistency of analysis across items or at different points in time.

3. Wakuluk is *most likely* to make significant adjustments to her estimate of the future growth trend for which of the following countries?
   A. Country Y only
   B. Country Z only
   C. Countries Y and Z

4. Based on Exhibit 1 and Wakuluk's assumptions about short-term rates and expected inflation, short-term rates in Country X are *most likely* to be:
   A. low and bottoming.
   B. approaching a peak.
   C. above average and rising.

5. Based on Exhibit 1, what capital market effect is Country Z *most likely* to experience in the short-term?
   A. Cyclical assets attract investors.
   B. Monetary policy becomes restrictive.
   C. The yield curve steepens substantially.

6. Based on Observation 1, fiscal and monetary policies in Country Y will *most likely* lead to:
   A. low nominal rates.
   B. high nominal rates.
   C. either high or low nominal rates.

7. Based on Observation 2, what impact will the policy changes have on the trend rate of growth for Country Y?
   A. Negative
   B. Neutral
   C. Positive

8. Based on Observation 3, Wakuluk *most likely* expects Country Y's yield curve in the near term to:
   A. invert.
   B. flatten.
   C. steepen.

The following information relates to Questions 9–10

Jennifer Wuyan is an investment strategist responsible for developing long-term capital market expectations for an investment firm that invests in domestic equities. She presents a report to the firm's investment committee describing the statistical model used to formulate capital market expectations, which is based on a dividend discount method. In the report, she notes that in developing the model, she researched the historical data seeking to identify the relevant variables and determined the best source of data for the model. She also notes her interpretation of the current economic and market environment.

9. **Explain** what additional step(s) Wuyan should have taken in the process of setting capital market expectations.

   Wuyan reports that after repeatedly searching the most recent 10 years of data, she eventually identified variables that had a statistically significant relationship with equity returns. Wuyan used these variables to forecast equity returns. She documented, in a separate section of the report, a high correlation between nominal GDP and equity returns. Based on this noted high correlation, Wuyan concludes that nominal GDP predicts equity returns. Based on her statistical results, Wuyan expects equities to underperform over the next 12 months and recommends that the firm underweight equities.

Commenting on the report, John Tommanson, an investment adviser for the firm, suggests extending the starting point of the historical data back another 20 years to obtain more robust statistical results. Doing so would enable the analysis to include different economic and central bank policy environments. Tommanson is reluctant to underweight equities for his clients, citing the strong performance of equities over the last quarter, and believes the most recent quarterly data should be weighted more heavily in setting capital market expectations.

10. **Discuss** how *each* of the following forecasting challenges evident in Wuyan's report and in Tommanson's comments affects the setting of capital market expectations:
    i.   Status quo bias
    ii. Data-mining bias
    iii. Risk of regime change
    iv. Misinterpretation of correlation

Discuss how *each* of the following forecasting challenges evident in Wuyan's report and in Tommanson's comments affects the setting of capital market expectations:

Status quo bias
Data-mining bias
Risk of regime change
Misinterpretation of correlation

The following information relates to Questions 11–13

Jan Cambo is chief market strategist at a US asset management firm. While preparing a report for the upcoming investment committee meeting, Cambo updates her long-term forecast for US equity returns. As an input into her forecasting model, she uses the following long-term annualized forecasts from the firm's chief economist:

- Labor input will grow 0.5%.
- Labor productivity will grow 1.3%.
- Inflation will be 2.2%.
- Dividend yield will be 2.8%.

Based on these forecasts, Cambo predicts a long-term 9.0% annual equity return in the US market. Her forecast assumes no change in the share of profits in the economy, and she expects some contribution to equity returns from a change in the price-to-earnings ratio (P/E).

11. **Calculate** the implied contribution to Cambo's US equity return forecast from the expected change in the P/E.

At the investment committee meeting, the firm's chief economist predicts that the economy will enter the late expansion phase of the business cycle in the next 12 months.

12. **Discuss**, based on the chief economist's prediction, the implications for the following:
    i.   Bond yields
    ii. Equity returns
    iii. Short-term interest rates

Discuss, based on the chief economist's prediction, the implications for the following:

Bond yields
Equity returns
Short-term interest rates

Cambo compares her business cycle forecasting approach to the approach used by the chief economist. Cambo bases her equity market forecast on a time-series model using a composite index of leading indicators as the key input, whereas the chief economist uses a detailed econometric model to generate his economic forecasts.

13. **Discuss** strengths and weaknesses of the economic forecasting approaches used by Cambo and the chief economist.

Discuss strengths and weaknesses of the economic forecasting approaches used by Cambo and the chief economist.

	Cambo's Forecasting Approach	Chief Economist's Forecasting Approach
Strengths		
Weaknesses		

The following information relates to Questions 14–16

Robert Hadpret is the chief economist at Agree Partners, an asset management firm located in the developed country of Eastland. He has prepared an economic report on Eastland for the firm's asset allocation committee. Hadpret notes that the composite index of leading economic indicators has declined for three consecutive months and that the yield curve has inverted. Private sector borrowing is also projected to decline. Based on these recent events, Hadpret predicts an economic contraction and forecasts lower inflation and possibly deflation over the next 12 months.

Helen Smitherman, a portfolio manager at Agree, considers Hadpret's economic forecast when determining the tactical allocation for the firm's Balanced Fund (the fund). Smitherman notes that the fund has considerable exposure to real estate, shares of asset-intensive and commodity-producing firms, and high-quality debt. The fund's cash holdings are at cyclical lows.

14. **Discuss** the implications of Hadpret's inflation forecast on the expected returns of the fund's holdings of:
    i. cash.
    ii. bonds.
    iii. equities.
    iv. real estate.

Discuss the implications of Hadpret's inflation forecast on the expected returns of the fund's holdings of:

Cash
Bonds
Equities
Real Estate

In response to the projected cyclical decline in the Eastland economy and in private sector borrowing over the next year, Hadpret expects a change in the monetary and fiscal policy mix. He forecasts that the Eastland central bank will ease monetary policy. On the fiscal side, Hadpret expects the Eastland government to enact a substantial tax cut. As a result, Hadpret forecasts large government deficits that will be financed by the issuance of long-term government securities.

15. **Discuss** the relationship between the shape of the yield curve and the monetary and fiscal policy mix projected by Hadpret.

Currently, Eastland's currency is fixed relative to the currency of the country of Northland, and Eastland maintains policies that allow unrestricted capital flows. Hadpret examines the relationship between interest rates and exchange rates. He considers three possible scenarios for the Eastland economy:

Scenario 1:　Shift in policy restricting capital flows
Scenario 2:　Shift in policy allowing the currency to float
Scenario 3:　Shift in investor belief toward a lack of full credibility that the exchange rate will be fixed forever

16. **Discuss** how interest rate and exchange rate linkages between Eastland and Northland might change under *each* scenario.
    Note: Consider *each* scenario independently.

Discuss how interest rate and exchange rate linkages between Eastland and Northland might change under *each* scenario. (Note: Consider *each* scenario independently.)

Scenario 1
Scenario 2
Scenario 3

CHAPTER 4

CAPITAL MARKET EXPECTATIONS, PART 2: FORECASTING ASSET CLASS RETURNS

LEARNING OUTCOMES

The candidate should be able to:

- discuss approaches to setting expectations for fixed-income returns;
- discuss risks faced by investors in emerging market fixed-income securities and the country risk analysis techniques used to evaluate emerging market economies;
- discuss approaches to setting expectations for equity investment market returns;
- discuss risks faced by investors in emerging market equity securities;
- explain how economic and competitive factors can affect expectations for real estate investment markets and sector returns;
- discuss major approaches to forecasting exchange rates;
- discuss methods of forecasting volatility;
- recommend and justify changes in the component weights of a global investment portfolio based on trends and expected changes in macroeconomic factors.

SUMMARY

The following are the main points covered in the chapter.

- The choice among forecasting techniques is effectively a choice of the information on which forecasts will be conditioned and how that information will be incorporated into the forecasts.
- The formal forecasting tools most commonly used in forecasting capital market returns fall into three broad categories: statistical methods, discounted cash flow models, and risk premium models.
- Sample statistics, especially the sample mean, are subject to substantial estimation error.
- Shrinkage estimation combines two estimates (or sets of estimates) into a more precise estimate.
- Time-series estimators, which explicitly incorporate dynamics, may summarize historical data well without providing insight into the underlying drivers of forecasts.
- Discounted cash flow models are used to estimate the required return implied by an asset's current price.
- The risk premium approach expresses expected return as the sum of the risk-free rate of interest and one or more risk premiums.
- There are three methods for modeling risk premiums: equilibrium models, such as the CAPM; factor models; and building blocks.
- The DCF method is the only one that is precise enough to use in support of trades involving individual fixed-income securities.
- There are three main methods for developing expected returns for fixed-income asset classes: DCF, building blocks, and inclusion in an equilibrium model.
- As a forecast of bond return, YTM, the most commonly quoted metric, can be improved by incorporating the impact of yield changes on reinvestment of cash flows and valuation at the investment horizon.
- The building blocks for fixed-income expected returns are the short-term default-free rate, the term premium, the credit premium, and the liquidity premium.
- Term premiums are roughly proportional to duration, whereas credit premiums tend to be larger at the short end of the curve.
- Both term premiums and credit premiums are positively related to the slope of the yield curve.
- Credit spreads reflect both the credit premium (i.e., additional expected return) and expected losses due to default.
- A baseline estimate of the liquidity premium can be based on the yield spread between the highest-quality issuer in a market (usually the sovereign) and the next highest-quality large issuer (often a government agency).
- Emerging market debt exposes investors to heightened risk with respect to both ability to pay and willingness to pay, which can be associated with the economy and political/legal weaknesses, respectively.
- The Grinold–Kroner model decomposes the expected return on equities into three components: (1) expected cash flow return, composed of the dividend yield minus the rate of change in shares outstanding, (2) expected return due to nominal earnings growth, and (3) expected repricing return, reflecting the rate of change in the P/E.

- Forecasting the equity premium directly is just as difficult as projecting the absolute level of equity returns, so the building block approach provides little, if any, specific insight with which to improve equity return forecasts.
- The Singer–Terhaar version of the international capital asset pricing model combines a global CAPM equilibrium that assumes full market integration with expected returns for each asset class based on complete segmentation.
- Emerging market equities expose investors to the same underlying risks as emerging market debt does: more fragile economies, less stable political and policy frameworks, and weaker legal protections.
- Emerging market investors need to pay particular attention to the ways in which the value of their ownership claims might be expropriated. Among the areas of concern are standards of corporate governance, accounting and disclosure standards, property rights laws, and checks and balances on governmental actions.
- Historical return data for real estate is subject to substantial smoothing, which biases standard volatility estimates downward and distorts correlations with other asset classes. Meaningful analysis of real estate as an asset class requires explicit handling of this data issue.
- Real estate is subject to boom–bust cycles that both drive and are driven by the business cycle.
- The cap rate, defined as net operating income in the current period divided by the property value, is the standard valuation metric for commercial real estate.
- A model similar to the Grinold–Kroner model can be applied to estimate the expected return on real estate:

$$E(R_{re}) = \text{Cap rate} + \text{NOI growth rate} - \%\Delta\text{Cap rate}$$

- There is a clear pattern of higher cap rates for riskier property types, lower-quality properties, and less attractive locations.
- Real estate expected returns contain all the standard building block risk premiums:
  - Term premium: As a very long-lived asset with relatively stable cash flows, income-producing real estate has a high duration.
  - Credit premium: A fixed-term lease is like a corporate bond issued by the leaseholder and secured by the property.
  - Equity premium: Owners bear the risk of property value fluctuations, as well as risk associated with rent growth, lease renewal, and vacancies.
  - Liquidity premium: Real estate trades infrequently and is costly to transact.

- Currency exchange rates are especially difficult to forecast because they are tied to governments, financial systems, legal systems, and geographies. Forecasting exchange rates requires identification and assessment of the forces that are likely to exert the most influence.
- Provided they can be financed, trade flows do not usually exert a significant impact on exchange rates. International capital flows are typically larger and more volatile than trade-financing flows.
- PPP is a poor predictor of exchange rate movements over short to intermediate horizons but is a better guide to currency movements over progressively longer multi-year horizons.
- The extent to which the current account balance influences the exchange rate depends primarily on whether it is likely to be persistent and, if so, whether it can be sustained.

- Capital seeks the highest risk-adjusted expected return. In a world of perfect capital mobility, in the long run, the exchange rate will be driven to the point at which the expected percentage change equals the "excess" risk-adjusted expected return on the portfolio of assets denominated in the domestic currency over that of the portfolio of assets denominated in the foreign currency. However, in the short run, there can be an exchange rate overshoot in the opposite direction as hot money chases higher returns.
- Carry trades are profitable on average, which is contrary to the predictions of uncovered interest rate parity.
- Each country/currency has a unique portfolio of assets that makes up part of the global "market portfolio." Exchange rates provide an across-the-board mechanism for adjusting the relative sizes of these portfolios to match investors' desire to hold them.
- The portfolio balance perspective implies that exchange rates adjust in response to changes in the relative sizes and compositions of the aggregate portfolios denominated in each currency.
- The sample variance–covariance matrix is an unbiased estimate of the true VCV structure; that is, it will be correct on average.
- There are two main problems with using the sample VCV matrix as an estimate/forecast of the true VCV matrix: It cannot be used for large numbers of asset classes, and it is subject to substantial sampling error.
- Linear factor models impose structure on the VCV matrix that allows them to handle very large numbers of asset classes. The drawback is that the VCV matrix is biased and inconsistent unless the assumed structure is true.
- Shrinkage estimation of the VCV matrix is a weighted average of the sample VCV matrix and a target VCV matrix that reflects assumed "prior" knowledge of the true VCV structure.
- Failure to adjust for the impact of smoothing in observed return data for real estate and other private assets will almost certainly lead to distorted portfolio analysis and hence poor asset allocation decisions.
- Financial asset returns exhibit volatility clustering, evidenced by periods of high and low volatilities. ARCH models were developed to address these time-varying volatilities.
- One of the simplest and most used ARCH models represents today's variance as a linear combination of yesterday's variance and a new "shock" to volatility. With appropriate parameter values, the model exhibits the volatility clustering characteristic of financial asset returns.

PRACTICE PROBLEMS

1. An investor is considering adding three new securities to her internationally focused fixed-income portfolio. She considers the following non-callable securities:
   - 1-year government bond
   - 10-year government bond
   - 10-year BBB rated corporate bond

   She plans to invest equally in all three securities being analyzed or will invest in none of them at this time. She will only make the added investment provided that the expected spread/premium of the equally weighted investment is at least 1.5 percent (150bp) over the 1-year government bond. She has gathered the following information:

Risk-free interest rate (1-year, incorporating 2.6% inflation expectation)	3.8%
Term premium (10-year vs. 1-year government bond)	1%
10-year BBB credit premium (over 10-year government bond)	75bp
Estimated liquidity premium on 10-year corporate bonds	55bp

Using only the information given, address the following problems using the risk premium approach:

A. Calculate the expected return that an equal-weighted investment in the three securities could provide.

B. Calculate the expected total risk premium of the three securities and determine the investor's probable course of action.

2. Jo Akumba's portfolio is invested in a range of developed market fixed-income securities. She asks her adviser about the possibility of diversifying her investments to include emerging and frontier markets government and corporate fixed-income securities. Her adviser makes the following comment regarding risk:

"All emerging and frontier market fixed-income securities pose economic, political, and legal risk. Economic risks arise from the fact that emerging market countries have poor fiscal discipline, rely on foreign borrowing, have less diverse tax base, and significant dependence on specific industries. They are susceptible to capital flight. Their ability to pay is limited. In addition, weak property rights, weak enforcement of contract laws, and political instability pose hazards for emerging markets debt investors."

Discuss the statement made.

3. An Australian investor currently holds a A$240 million equity portfolio. He is considering rebalancing the portfolio based on an assessment of the risk and return prospects facing the Australian economy. Information relating to the Australian investment markets and the economy has been collected in the following table:

10-Year Historical	Current	Capital Market Expectations
Average government bond yield: 2.8%	10-year government bond yield: 2.3%	Expected annual inflation: 2.3%
Average annual equity return: 4.6%	Year-over-year equity return: −9.4%	Expected equity market P/E: 14.0×
Average annual inflation rate: 2.3%	Year-over-year inflation rate: 2.1%	Expected annual income return: 2.4%
Equity market P/E (beginning of period): 15×	Current equity market P/E: 14.5×	Expected annual real earnings growth: 5.0%
Average annual dividend income return: 2.6%		
Average annual real earnings growth: 6.0%		

Using the information in the table, address the following problems:

A. Calculate the historical Australian equity risk premium using the "equity-vs-bonds" premium method.

B. Calculate the expected annual equity return using the Grinold–Kroner model (assume no change in the number of shares outstanding).

C. Using your answer to Part B, calculate the expected annual equity risk premium.

4. An analyst is reviewing various asset alternatives and is presented with the following information relating to the broad equity market of Switzerland and various industries within the Swiss market that are of particular investment interest.

Expected risk premium for overall global investable market (GIM) portfolio	3.5%
Expected standard deviation for the GIM portfolio	8.5%
Expected standard deviation for Swiss Health Care Industry equity investments	12.0%
Expected standard deviation for Swiss Watch Industry equity investments	6.0%
Expected standard deviation for Swiss Consumer Products Industry equity investments	7.5%

Assume that the Swiss market is perfectly integrated with the world markets.
Swiss Health Care has a correlation of 0.7 with the GIM portfolio.
Swiss Watch has a correlation of 0.8 with the GIM portfolio.
Swiss Consumer Products has a correlation of 0.8 with the GIM portfolio.

A. Basing your answers only upon the data presented in the table above and using the international capital asset pricing model—in particular, the Singer–Terhaar approach—estimate the expected risk premium for the following:
    i.   Swiss Health Care Industry
    ii. Swiss Watch Industry
    iii. Swiss Consumer Products Industry

B. Judge which industry is most attractive from a valuation perspective.

5. Identify risks faced by investors in emerging market equities over and above those that are faced by fixed-income investors in such markets.

6. Describe the main issues that arise when conducting historical analysis of real estate returns.

7. An analyst at a real estate investment management firm seeks to establish expectations for rate of return for properties in the industrial sector over the next year. She has obtained the following information:

Current industrial sector capitalization rate ("cap" rate)	5.7%
Expected cap rate at the end of the period	5.5%
NOI growth rate (real)	1%
Inflation expectation	1.5%

Estimate the expected return from the industrial sector properties based on the data provided.

8. A client has asked his adviser to explain the key considerations in forecasting exchange rates. The adviser's firm uses two broad complementary approaches when setting expectations for exchange rate movements, namely, focus on trade in goods and services and, secondly, focus on capital flows. Identify the main considerations that the adviser should explain to the client under the two approaches.

9. Looking independently at each of the economic observations below, indicate the country where an analyst would expect to see a strengthening currency for each observation.

	Country X	Country Y
Expected inflation over next year	2.0%	3.0%
Short-term (1-month) government rate	Decrease	Increase
Expected (forward-looking) GDP growth over next year	2.0%	3.3%
New national laws have been passed that enable foreign direct investment in real estate/financial companies	Yes	No
Current account surplus (deficit)	8%	−1%

10. Fap is a small country whose currency is the Fip. Three years ago, the exchange rate was considered to be reflecting purchasing power parity (PPP). Since then, the country's inflation has exceeded inflation in the other countries by about 5% per annum. The Fip exchange rate, however, remained broadly unchanged.

What would you have expected the Fip exchange rate to show if PPP prevailed?

Are Fips over- or undervalued, according to PPP?

The following information relates to Questions 11–18

Richard Martin is chief investment officer for the Trunch Foundation (the foundation), which has a large, globally diversified investment portfolio. Martin meets with the foundation's fixed-income and real estate portfolio managers to review expected return forecasts and potential investments, as well as to consider short-term modifications to asset weights within the total fund strategic asset allocation.

Martin asks the real estate portfolio manager to discuss the performance characteristics of real estate. The real estate portfolio manager makes the following statements:

Statement 1: Adding traded REIT securities to an equity portfolio should substantially improve the portfolio's diversification over the next year.

Statement 2: Traded REIT securities are more highly correlated with direct real estate and less highly correlated with equities over multi-year horizons.

Martin looks over the long-run valuation metrics the manager is using for commercial real estate, shown in Exhibit 1.

EXHIBIT 1   Commercial Real Estate Valuation Metrics

Cap Rate	GDP Growth Rate
4.70%	4.60%

The real estate team uses an in-house model for private real estate to estimate the true volatility of returns over time. The model assumes that the current observed return equals the weighted average of the current true return and the previous observed return. Because the true return is not observable, the model assumes a relationship between true returns and observable REIT index returns; therefore, it uses REIT index returns as proxies for both the unobservable current true return and the previous observed return.

Martin asks the fixed-income portfolio manager to review the foundation's bond portfolios. The existing aggregate bond portfolio is broadly diversified in domestic and international developed markets. The first segment of the portfolio to be reviewed is the domestic sovereign portfolio. The bond manager notes that there is a market consensus that the domestic yield curve will likely experience a single 20 bp increase in the near term as a result of monetary tightening and then remain relatively flat and stable for the next three years. Martin then reviews duration and yield measures for the short-term domestic sovereign bond portfolio in Exhibit 2.

EXHIBIT 2   Short-Term Domestic Sovereign Bond Portfolio

Macaulay Duration	Modified Duration	Yield to Maturity
3.00	2.94	2.00%

The discussion turns to the international developed fixed-income market. The foundation invested in bonds issued by Country XYZ, a foreign developed country. XYZ's sovereign yield curve is currently upward sloping, and the yield spread between 2-year and 10-year XYZ bonds is 100 bps.

The fixed-income portfolio manager tells Martin that he is interested in a domestic market corporate bond issued by Zeus Manufacturing Corporation (ZMC). ZMC has just been downgraded two steps by a major credit rating agency. In addition to expected monetary actions that will raise short-term rates, the yield spread between three-year sovereign bonds and the next highest-quality government agency bond widened by 10 bps.

Although the foundation's fixed-income portfolios have focused primarily on developed markets, the portfolio manager presents data in Exhibit 3 on two emerging markets for Martin to consider. Both economies increased exports of their mineral resources over the last decade.

EXHIBIT 3   Emerging Market Data

Factor	Emerging Republic A	Emerging Republic B
Fiscal deficit/GDP	6.50%	8.20%
Debt/GDP	90.10%	104.20%
Current account deficit	5.20% of GDP	7.10% of GDP
Foreign exchange reserves	90.30% of short-term debt	70.10% of short-term debt

The fixed-income portfolio manager also presents information on a new investment opportunity in an international developed market. The team is considering the bonds of Xdelp, a large energy exploration and production company. Both the domestic and international markets are experiencing synchronized growth in GDP midway between the trough and the peak of the business cycle. The foreign country's government has displayed a disciplined approach to maintaining stable monetary and fiscal policies and has experienced a rising current account surplus and an appreciating currency. It is expected that with the improvements in free cash flow and earnings, the credit rating of the Xdelp bonds will be upgraded. Martin refers to the foundation's asset allocation policy in Exhibit 4 before making any changes to either the fixed-income or real estate portfolios.

EXHIBIT 4   Trunch Foundation Strategic Asset Allocation—Select Data

Asset Class	Minimum Weight	Maximum Weight	Actual Weight
Fixed income—Domestic	40.00%	80.00%	43.22%
Fixed income—International	5.00%	10.00%	6.17%
Fixed income—Emerging markets	0.00%	2.00%	0.00%
Alternatives—Real estate	2.00%	6.00%	3.34%

11. Which of the real estate portfolio manager's statements is correct?
    A. Only Statement 1
    B. Only Statement 2
    C. Both Statement 1 and Statement 2

12. Based only on Exhibit 1, the long-run expected return for commercial real estate:
    A. is approximately double the cap rate.
    B. incorporates a cap rate greater than the discount rate.
    C. needs to include the cap rate's anticipated rate of change.

13. Based on the private real estate model developed to estimate return volatility, the true variance is *most likely*:
    A. lower than the variance of the observed data.
    B. approximately equal to the variance of the observed data.
    C. greater than the variance of the observed data.

14. Based on Exhibit 2 and the anticipated effects of the monetary policy change, the expected annual return over a three-year investment horizon will *most likely* be:
    A. lower than 2.00%.
    B. approximately equal to 2.00%.
    C. greater than 2.00%.

15. Based on the building block approach to fixed-income returns, the dominant source of the yield spread for Country XYZ is *most likely* the:
    A. term premium.
    B. credit premium.
    C. liquidity premium.

16. Using the building block approach, the required rate of return for the ZMC bond will *most likely*:
    A. increase based on the change in the credit premium.
    B. decrease based on the change in the default-free rate.
    C. decrease based on the change in the liquidity premium.

17. Based only on Exhibit 3, the foundation would *most likely* consider buying bonds issued by:
    A. only Emerging Republic A.
    B. only Emerging Republic B.
    C. neither Emerging Republic A nor Emerging Republic B.

18. Based only on Exhibits 3 and 4 and the information provided by the portfolio managers, the action *most likely* to enhance returns is to:
    A. decrease existing investments in real estate by 2.00%.
    B. initiate a commitment to emerging market debt of 1.00%.
    C. increase the investments in international market bonds by 1.00%.

The following information relates to Questions 19–26

Judith Bader is a senior analyst for a company that specializes in managing international developed and emerging markets equities. Next week, Bader must present proposed changes to client portfolios to the Investment Committee, and she is preparing a presentation to support the views underlying her recommendations.

Bader begins by analyzing portfolio risk. She decides to forecast a variance–covariance matrix (VCV) for 20 asset classes, using 10 years of monthly returns and incorporating both the sample statistics and the factor-model methods. To mitigate the impact of estimation error, Bader is considering combining the results of the two methods in an alternative target VCV matrix, using shrinkage estimation.

Bader asks her research assistant to comment on the two approaches and the benefits of applying shrinkage estimation. The assistant makes the following statements:

Statement 1: Shrinkage estimation of VCV matrices will decrease the efficiency of the estimates versus the sample VCV matrix.

Statement 2: Your proposed approach for estimating the VCV matrix will not be reliable because a sample VCV matrix is biased and inconsistent.

Statement 3: A factor-based VCV matrix approach may result in some portfolios that erroneously appear to be riskless if any asset returns can be completely determined by the common factors or some of the factors are redundant.

Bader then uses the Singer–Terhaar model and the final shrinkage-estimated VCV matrix to determine the equilibrium expected equity returns for all international asset classes by country. Three of the markets under consideration are located in Country A (developed market), Country B (emerging market), and Country C (emerging market). Bader projects that in relation to the global market, the equity market in Country A will remain highly integrated, the equity market in Country B will become more segmented, and the equity market in Country C will become more fully integrated.

Next, Bader applies the Grinold–Kroner model to estimate the expected equity returns for the various markets under consideration. For Country A, Bader assumes a very long-term corporate earnings growth rate of 4% per year (equal to the expected nominal GDP growth rate), a 2% rate of net share repurchases for Country A's equities, and an expansion rate for P/E multiples of 0.5% per year.

In reviewing Countries B and C, Bader's research assistant comments that emerging markets are especially risky owing to issues related to politics, competition, and accounting standards. As an example, Bader and her assistant discuss the risk implications of the following information related to Country B:

- Experiencing declining per capita income
- Expected to continue its persistent current account deficit below 2% of GDP
- Transitioning to International Financial Reporting Standards, with full convergence scheduled to be completed within two years

Bader shifts her focus to currency expectations relative to clients' base currency and summarizes her assumptions in Exhibit 1.

EXHIBIT 1   Baseline Assumptions for Currency Forecasts

	Country A	Country B	Country C
Historical current account	Persistent current account deficit of 5% of GDP	Persistent current account deficit of 2% of GDP	Persistent current account surplus of 2% of GDP
Expectation for secular trend in current account	Rising current account deficit	Narrowing current account deficit	Rising current account surplus
Long-term inflation expectation relative to global inflation	Expected to rise	Expected to keep pace	Expected to fall
Capital flows	Steady inflows	Hot money flowing out	Hot money flowing in

During a conversation about Exhibit 1, Bader and her research assistant discuss the composition of each country's currency portfolio and the potential for triggering a crisis. Bader notes that some flows and holdings are more or less supportive of the currency, stating that investments in private equity make up the majority of Country A's currency portfolio, investments in public equity make up the majority of Country B's currency portfolio, and investments in public debt make up the majority of Country C's currency portfolio.

19. Which of the following statements made by Bader's research assistant is correct?
    A. Statement 1
    B. Statement 2
    C. Statement 3

20. Based on expectations for changes in integration with the global market, all else being equal, the Singer–Terhaar model implies that Bader should shift capital from Country A to:
    A. only Country B.
    B. only Country C.
    C. both Countries B and C.

21. Using the Grinold–Kroner model, which of the following assumptions for forecasting Country A's expected equity returns is plausible for the very long run?
    A. Rate of net share repurchases
    B. Corporate earnings growth rate
    C. Expansion rate for P/E multiples

22. Based only on the emerging markets discussion, developments in which of the following areas *most likely* signal increasing risk for Country B's equity market?
    A. Politics
    B. Competitiveness
    C. Accounting standards

23. Based on Bader's expectations for current account secular trends as shown in Exhibit 1, Bader should reallocate capital, all else being equal, from:
    A. Country A to Country C.
    B. Country B to Country A.
    C. Country C to Country A.

24. Based on Bader's inflation expectations as shown in Exhibit 1, purchasing power parity implies that which of the following countries' currencies should depreciate, all else being equal?
    A. Country A
    B. Country B
    C. Country C

25. Based on Exhibit 1, which country's central bank is *most likely* to buy domestic bonds near term to sterilize the impact of money flows on domestic liquidity?
    A. Country A
    B. Country B
    C. Country C

26. Based on the composition of each country's currency portfolio, which country is most vulnerable to a potential crisis?
    A. Country A
    B. Country B
    C. Country C

CHAPTER 5

OVERVIEW OF ASSET ALLOCATION

LEARNING OUTCOMES

The candidate should be able to:

- describe elements of effective investment governance and investment governance considerations in asset allocation;
- prepare an economic balance sheet for a client and interpret its implications for asset allocation;
- compare the investment objectives of asset-only, liability-relative, and goals-based asset allocation approaches;
- contrast concepts of risk relevant to asset-only, liability-relative, and goals-based asset allocation approaches;
- explain how asset classes are used to represent exposures to systematic risk and discuss criteria for asset class specification;
- explain the use of risk factors in asset allocation and their relation to traditional asset class–based approaches;
- select and justify an asset allocation based on an investor's objectives and constraints;
- describe the use of the global market portfolio as a baseline portfolio in asset allocation;
- discuss strategic implementation choices in asset allocation, including passive/active choices and vehicles for implementing passive and active mandates;
- discuss strategic considerations in rebalancing asset allocations.

SUMMARY

This chapter has introduced the subject of asset allocation. Among the points made are the following:

- Effective investment governance ensures that decisions are made by individuals or groups with the necessary skills and capacity and involves articulating the long- and short-term objectives of the investment program; effectively allocating decision rights and responsibilities among the functional units in the governance hierarchy; taking account of their knowledge, capacity, time, and position on the governance hierarchy; specifying processes for developing and approving the investment policy statement, which will govern the day-to-day operation of the investment program; specifying processes for developing and approving the program's strategic asset allocation; establishing a reporting framework to monitor the program's progress toward the agreed-on goals and objectives; and periodically undertaking a governance audit.
- The economic balance sheet includes non-financial assets and liabilities that can be relevant for choosing the best asset allocation for an investor's financial portfolio.
- The investment objectives of asset-only asset allocation approaches focus on the asset side of the economic balance sheet; approaches with a liability-relative orientation focus on funding liabilities; and goals-based approaches focus on achieving financial goals.
- The risk concepts relevant to asset-only asset allocation approaches focus on asset risk; those of liability-relative asset allocation focus on risk in relation to paying liabilities; and a goals-based approach focuses on the probabilities of not achieving financial goals.
- Asset classes are the traditional units of analysis in asset allocation and reflect systematic risks with varying degrees of overlap.
- Assets within an asset class should be relatively homogeneous; asset classes should be mutually exclusive; asset classes should be diversifying; asset classes as a group should make up a preponderance of the world's investable wealth; asset classes selected for investment should have the capacity to absorb a meaningful proportion of an investor's portfolio.
- Risk factors are associated with non-diversifiable (i.e., systematic) risk and are associated with an expected return premium. The price of an asset and/or asset class may reflect more than one risk factor, and complicated spread positions may be necessary to identify and isolate particular risk factors. Their use as units of analysis in asset allocation is driven by considerations of controlling systematic risk exposures.
- The global market portfolio represents a highly diversified asset allocation that can serve as a baseline asset allocation in an asset-only approach.
- There are two dimensions of passive/active choices. One dimension relates to the management of the strategic asset allocation itself—for example, whether to deviate from it tactically or not. The second dimension relates to passive and active implementation choices in investing the allocation to a given asset class. Tactical and dynamic asset allocation relate to the first dimension; active and passive choices for implementing allocations to asset classes relate to the second dimension.
- Risk budgeting addresses the question of which types of risks to take and how much of each to take. Active risk budgeting addresses the question of how much benchmark-relative risk an investor is willing to take. At the level of the overall asset allocation, active risk can be defined relative to the strategic asset allocation benchmark. At the level of individual asset classes, active risk can be defined relative to the benchmark proxy.

- Rebalancing is the discipline of adjusting portfolio weights to more closely align with the strategic asset allocation. Rebalancing approaches include calendar-based and range-based rebalancing. Calendar-based rebalancing rebalances the portfolio to target weights on a periodic basis. Range-based rebalancing sets rebalancing thresholds or trigger points around target weights. The ranges may be fixed width, percentage based, or volatility based. Range-based rebalancing permits tighter control of the asset mix compared with calendar rebalancing.
- Strategic considerations in rebalancing include transaction costs, risk aversion, correlations among asset classes, volatility, and beliefs concerning momentum, taxation, and asset class liquidity.

PRACTICE PROBLEMS

The following information relates to Questions 1–8

Meg and Cramer Law, a married couple aged 42 and 44, respectively, are meeting with their new investment adviser, Daniel Raye. The Laws have worked their entire careers at Whorton Solutions (WS), a multinational technology company. The Laws have two teenage children who will soon begin college.

Raye reviews the Laws' current financial position. The Laws have an investment portfolio consisting of $800,000 in equities and $450,000 in fixed-income instruments. Raye notes that 80% of the equity portfolio consists of shares of WS. The Laws also own real estate valued at $400,000, with $225,000 in mortgage debt. Raye estimates the Laws' pre-retirement earnings from WS have a total present value of $1,025,000. He estimates the Laws' future expected consumption expenditures have a total present value of $750,000.

The Laws express a very strong desire to fund their children's college education expenses, which have an estimated present value of $275,000. The Laws also plan to fund an endowment at their alma mater in 20 years, which has an estimated present value of $500,000. The Laws tell Raye they want a high probability of success funding the endowment. Raye uses this information to prepare an economic balance sheet for the Laws.

In reviewing a financial plan written by the Laws' previous adviser, Raye notices the following asset class specifications.

Equity:	US equities
Debt:	Global investment-grade corporate bonds and real estate
Derivatives:	Primarily large-capitalization foreign equities

The previous adviser's report notes the asset class returns on equity and derivatives are highly correlated. The report also notes the asset class returns on debt have a low correlation with equity and derivative returns.

Raye is concerned that the asset allocation approach followed by the Laws' previous financial adviser resulted in an overlap in risk factors among asset classes for the portfolio. Raye plans to address this by examining the portfolio's sensitivity to various risk factors, such as inflation, liquidity, and volatility, to determine the desired exposure to each factor.

Raye concludes that a portfolio of 75% global equities and 25% bonds reflects an appropriate balance of expected return and risk for the Laws with respect to a 20-year time horizon for most moderately important goals. Raye recommends the Laws follow a goals-based approach to asset allocation and offers three possible portfolios for the Laws to consider. Selected data on the three portfolios are presented in Exhibit 1.

EXHIBIT 1   Proposed Portfolio Allocations for the Law Family

	Cash	Fixed Income	Global Equities	Diversifying Strategies*
Portfolio 1	35%	55%	10%	0%
Portfolio 2	10%	15%	65%	10%
Portfolio 3	10%	30%	40%	20%

*Diversifying strategies consists of hedge funds.

Raye uses a cost–benefit approach to rebalancing and recommends that global equities have a wider rebalancing range than the other asset classes.

1. Using the economic balance sheet approach, the Laws' economic net worth is *closest* to:
   A. $925,000.
   B. $1,425,000.
   C. $1,675,000.

2. Using an economic balance sheet, which of the Laws' current financial assets is *most concerning* from an asset allocation perspective?
   A. Equities
   B. Real estate
   C. Fixed income

3. Raye believes the previous adviser's specification for debt is incorrect given that, for purposes of asset allocation, asset classes should be:
   A. diversifying.
   B. mutually exclusive.
   C. relatively homogeneous.

4. Raye believes the previous adviser's asset class specifications for equity and derivatives are inappropriate given that, for purposes of asset allocation, asset classes should be:
   A. diversifying.
   B. mutually exclusive.
   C. relatively homogeneous.

5. To address his concern regarding the previous adviser's asset allocation approach, Raye should assess the Laws' portfolio using:
   A. a homogeneous and mutually exclusive asset class–based risk analysis.
   B. a multifactor risk model to control systematic risk factors in asset allocation.
   C. an asset class–based asset allocation approach to construct a diversified portfolio.

6. Based on Exhibit 1, which portfolio *best* meets the Laws' education goal for their children?
   A. Portfolio 1
   B. Portfolio 2
   C. Portfolio 3

7. Based on Exhibit 1, which portfolio *best* meets the Laws' goal to fund an endowment for their alma mater?
   A. Portfolio 1
   B. Portfolio 2
   C. Portfolio 3

8. Raye's approach to rebalancing global equities is consistent with:
   A. the Laws' being risk averse.
   B. global equities' having higher transaction costs than other asset classes.
   C. global equities' having lower correlations with other asset classes.

CHAPTER **6**

PRINCIPLES OF ASSET ALLOCATION

LEARNING OUTCOMES

The candidate should be able to:

- describe and critique the use of mean–variance optimization in asset allocation;
- recommend and justify an asset allocation using mean–variance optimization;
- interpret and critique an asset allocation in relation to an investor's economic balance sheet;
- discuss asset class liquidity considerations in asset allocation;
- explain absolute and relative risk budgets and their use in determining and implementing an asset allocation;
- describe how client needs and preferences regarding investment risks can be incorporated into asset allocation;
- discuss the use of Monte Carlo simulation and scenario analysis to evaluate the robustness of an asset allocation;
- describe the use of investment factors in constructing and analyzing an asset allocation;
- recommend and justify an asset allocation based on the global market portfolio;
- describe and evaluate characteristics of liabilities that are relevant to asset allocation;
- discuss approaches to liability-relative asset allocation;
- recommend and justify a liability-relative asset allocation;
- recommend and justify an asset allocation using a goals-based approach;
- describe and critique heuristic and other approaches to asset allocation;
- discuss factors affecting rebalancing policy.

SUMMARY

This chapter has surveyed how appropriate asset allocations can be determined to meet the needs of a variety of investors. Among the major points made have been the following:

- The objective function of asset-only mean–variance optimization is to maximize the expected return of the asset mix minus a penalty that depends on risk aversion and the expected variance of the asset mix.
- Criticisms of MVO include the following:
- The outputs (asset allocations) are highly sensitive to small changes in the inputs.
- The asset allocations are highly concentrated in a subset of the available asset classes.
- Investors are often concerned with characteristics of asset class returns such as skewness and kurtosis that are not accounted for in MVO.
- While the asset allocations may appear diversified across assets, the sources of risk may not be diversified.
- MVO allocations may have no direct connection to the factors affecting any liability or consumption streams.
- MVO is a single-period framework that tends to ignore trading/rebalancing costs and taxes.
- Deriving expected returns by reverse optimization or by reverse optimization tilted toward an investor's views on asset returns (the Black–Litterman model) is one means of addressing the tendency of MVO to produce efficient portfolios that are not well diversified.
- Placing constraints on asset class weights to prevent extremely concentrated portfolios and resampling inputs are other ways of addressing the same concern.
- For some relatively illiquid asset classes, a satisfactory proxy may not be available; including such asset classes in the optimization may therefore be problematic.
- Risk budgeting is a means of making optimal use of risk in the pursuit of return. A risk budget is optimal when the ratio of excess return to marginal contribution to total risk is the same for all assets in the portfolio.
- Characteristics of liabilities that affect asset allocation in liability-relative asset allocation include the following:
- Fixed versus contingent cash flows
- Legal versus quasi-liabilities
- Duration and convexity of liability cash flows
- Value of liabilities as compared with the size of the sponsoring organization
- Factors driving future liability cash flows (inflation, economic conditions, interest rates, risk premium)
- Timing considerations, such longevity risk
- Regulations affecting liability cash flow calculations
- Approaches to liability-relative asset allocation include surplus optimization, a hedging/return-seeking portfolios approach, and an integrated asset–liability approach.
- Surplus optimization involves MVO applied to surplus returns
- A hedging/return-seeking portfolios approach assigns assets to one of two portfolios. The objective of the hedging portfolio is to hedge the investor's liability stream. Any remaining funds are invested in the return-seeking portfolio.
- An integrated asset–liability approach integrates and jointly optimizes asset and liability decisions.

- A goals-based asset allocation process combines into an overall portfolio a number of sub-portfolios, each of which is designed to fund an individual goal with its own time horizon and required probability of success.
- In the implementation, there are two fundamental parts to the asset allocation process. The first centers on the creation of portfolio modules, while the second relates to the identification of client goals and the matching of these goals to the appropriate sub-portfolios to which suitable levels of capital are allocated.
- Other approaches to asset allocation include "120 minus your age," 60/40 stocks/bonds, the endowment model, risk parity, and the $1/N$ rule.
- Disciplined rebalancing has tended to reduce risk while incrementally adding to returns. Interpretations of this empirical finding include that rebalancing earns a diversification return, that rebalancing earns a return from being short volatility, and that rebalancing earns a return to supplying liquidity to the market.
- Factors positively related to optimal corridor width include transaction costs, risk tolerance, and an asset class's correlation with the rest of the portfolio. The higher the correlation, the wider the optimal corridor, because when asset classes move in sync, further divergence from target weights is less likely.
- The volatility of the rest of the portfolio (outside of the asset class under consideration) is inversely related to optimal corridor width.
- An asset class's own volatility involves a trade-off between transaction costs and risk control. The width of the optimal tolerance band increases with transaction costs for volatility-based rebalancing.

PRACTICE PROBLEMS

The following information relates to questions 1–8

Megan Beade and Hanna Müller are senior analysts for a large, multi-divisional money management firm. Beade supports the institutional portfolio managers, and Müller does the same for the private wealth portfolio managers.

Beade reviews the asset allocation in Exhibit 1, derived from a mean–variance optimization (MVO) model for an institutional client, noting that details of the MVO are lacking.

EXHIBIT 1   Asset Allocation and Market Weights (in percent)

Asset Classes	Asset Allocation	Investable Global Market Weights
Cash	0	—
US bonds	30	17
US TIPS	0	3
Non-US bonds	0	22
Emerging market equity	25	5
Non-US developed equity	20	29
US small- and mid-cap equity	25	4
US large-cap equity	0	20

The firm's policy is to rebalance a portfolio when the asset class weight falls outside of a corridor around the target allocation. The width of each corridor is customized for each client and proportional to the target allocation. Beade recommends wider corridor widths for high-risk asset classes, narrower corridor widths for less liquid asset classes, and narrower corridor widths for taxable clients with high capital gains tax rates.

One client sponsors a defined benefit pension plan where the present value of the liabilities is $241 million and the market value of plan assets is $205 million. Beade expects interest rates to rise and both the present value of plan liabilities and the market value of plan assets to decrease by $25 million, changing the pension plan's funding ratio.

Beade uses a surplus optimization approach to liability-relative asset allocation based on the objective function

$$U_m^{LR} = E(R_{s,m}) - 0.005\lambda\sigma^2(R_{s,m})$$

where $E(R_{s,m})$ is the expected surplus return for portfolio m, λ is the risk aversion coefficient, and $\sigma^2(R_{s,m})$ is the variance of the surplus return. Beade establishes the expected surplus return and surplus variance for three different asset allocations, shown in Exhibit 2. Given $\lambda = 1.50$, she chooses the optimal asset mix.

EXHIBIT 2   Expected Surplus Return and Volatility for Three Portfolios

	Return	Standard Deviation
Portfolio 1	13.00%	24%
Portfolio 2	12.00%	18%
Portfolio 3	11.00%	19%

Client Haunani Kealoha has a large fixed obligation due in 10 years. Beade assesses that Kealoha has substantially more funds than are required to meet the fixed obligation. The client wants to earn a competitive risk-adjusted rate of return while maintaining a high level of certainty that there will be sufficient assets to meet the fixed obligation.

In the private wealth area, the firm has designed five sub-portfolios with differing asset allocations that are used to fund different client goals over a five-year horizon. Exhibit 3 shows the expected returns and volatilities of the sub-portfolios and the probabilities that the sub-portfolios will exceed an expected minimum return. Client Luis Rodríguez wants to satisfy two goals. Goal 1 requires a conservative portfolio providing the highest possible minimum return that will be met at least 95% of the time. Goal 2 requires a riskier portfolio that provides the highest minimum return that will be exceeded at least 85% of the time.

EXHIBIT 3   Characteristics of Sub-Portfolios

Sub-Portfolio	A	B	C	D	E
Expected return, in percent	4.60	5.80	7.00	8.20	9.40
Expected volatility, in percent	3.46	5.51	8.08	10.80	13.59
Required Success Rate	**Minimum Expected Return for Success Rate**				
99%	1.00	0.07	−1.40	−3.04	−4.74
95%	2.05	1.75	1.06	0.25	−0.60
90%	2.62	2.64	2.37	2.01	1.61
85%	3.00	3.25	3.26	3.19	3.10
75%	3.56	4.14	4.56	4.94	5.30

Müller uses a risk parity asset allocation approach with a client's four–asset class portfolio. The expected return of the domestic bond asset class is the lowest of the asset classes, and the returns of the domestic bond asset class have the lowest covariance with other asset class returns. Müller estimates the weight that should be placed on domestic bonds.

Müller and a client discuss other approaches to asset allocation that are not based on optimization models or goals-based models. Müller makes the following comments to the client:

Comment 1.   An advantage of the "120 minus your age" heuristic over the 60/40 stock/bond heuristic is that it incorporates an age-based stock/bond allocation.

Comment 2.   The Yale model emphasizes traditional investments and a commitment to active management.

Comment 3.   A client's asset allocation using the $1/N$ rule depends on the investment characteristics of each asset class.

1. The asset allocation in Exhibit 1 *most likely* resulted from a mean–variance optimization using:
   A. historical data.
   B. reverse optimization.
   C. Black–Litterman inputs.

2. For clients concerned about rebalancing-related transactions costs, which of Beade's suggested changes in the corridor width of the rebalancing policy is correct? The change with respect to:
   A. high-risk asset classes.
   B. less liquid asset classes.
   C. taxable clients with high capital gains tax rates.

3. Based on Beade's interest rate expectations, the pension plan's funding ratio will:
   A. decrease.
   B. remain unchanged.
   C. increase.

4. Based on Exhibit 2, which portfolio provides the greatest objective function expected value?
   A. Portfolio 1
   B. Portfolio 2
   C. Portfolio 3

5. The asset allocation approach most appropriate for client Kealoha is *best* described as:
   A. a surplus optimization approach.
   B. an integrated asset–liability approach.
   C. a hedging/return-seeking portfolios approach.

6. Based on Exhibit 3, which sub-portfolios *best* meet the two goals expressed by client Rodríguez?
   A. Sub-Portfolio A for Goal 1 and Sub-Portfolio C for Goal 2
   B. Sub-Portfolio B for Goal 1 and Sub-Portfolio C for Goal 2
   C. Sub-Portfolio E for Goal 1 and Sub-Portfolio A for Goal 2

7. In the risk parity asset allocation approach that Müller uses, the weight that Müller places on domestic bonds should be:
   A. less than 25%.
   B. equal to 25%.
   C. greater than 25%.

8. Which of Müller's comments about the other approaches to asset allocation is correct?
   A. Comment 1
   B. Comment 2
   C. Comment 3

The following information relates to questions 9–13

Investment adviser Carl Monteo determines client asset allocations using quantitative techniques such as mean–variance optimization (MVO) and risk budgets. Monteo is reviewing the allocations of three clients. Exhibit 1 shows the expected return and standard deviation of returns for three strategic asset allocations that apply to several of Monteo's clients.

EXHIBIT 1   Strategic Asset Allocation Alternatives

	Adviser's Forecasts	
Asset Allocation	Expected Return (%)	Standard Deviation of Returns (%)
A	10	12.0
B	8	8.0
C	6	2.0

Monteo interviews client Mary Perkins and develops a detailed assessment of her risk preference and capacity for risk, which is needed to apply MVO to asset allocation. Monteo estimates the risk aversion coefficient (λ) for Perkins to be 8 and uses the following utility function to determine a preferred asset allocation for Perkins:

$$U_m = E(R_m) - 0.005\lambda\sigma_m^2$$

Another client, Lars Velky, represents Velky Partners (VP), a large institutional investor with $500 million in investable assets. Velky is interested in adding less liquid asset classes, such as direct real estate, infrastructure, and private equity, to VP's portfolio. Velky and Monteo discuss the considerations involved in applying many of the common asset allocation techniques, such as MVO, to these asset classes. Before making any changes to the portfolio, Monteo asks Velky about his knowledge of risk budgeting. Velky makes the following statements:

Statement 1. An optimum risk budget minimizes total risk.
Statement 2. Risk budgeting decomposes total portfolio risk into its constituent parts.
Statement 3. An asset allocation is optimal from a risk-budgeting perspective when the ratio of excess return to marginal contribution to risk is different for all assets in the portfolio.

Monteo meets with a third client, Jayanta Chaterji, an individual investor. Monteo and Chaterji discuss mean–variance optimization. Chaterji expresses concern about using the output of MVOs for two reasons:

Criticism 1: The asset allocations are highly sensitive to changes in the model inputs.
Criticism 2: The asset allocations tend to be highly dispersed across all available asset classes.

Monteo and Chaterji also discuss other approaches to asset allocation. Chaterji tells Monteo that he understands the factor-based approach to asset allocation to have two key characteristics:

Characteristic 1. The factors commonly used in the factor-based approach generally have low correlations with the market and with each other.
Characteristic 2. The factors commonly used in the factor-based approach are typically different from the fundamental or structural factors used in multifactor models.

Monteo concludes the meeting with Chaterji after sharing his views on the factor-based approach.

9. Based on Exhibit 1 and the risk aversion coefficient, the preferred asset allocation for Perkins is:
    A. Asset Allocation A.
    B. Asset Allocation B.
    C. Asset Allocation C.

10. In their discussion of the asset classes that Velky is interested in adding to the VP portfolio, Monteo should tell Velky that:
    A. these asset classes can be readily diversified to eliminate idiosyncratic risk.
    B. indexes are available for these asset classes that do an outstanding job of representing the performance characteristics of the asset classes.
    C. the risk and return characteristics associated with actual investment vehicles for these asset classes are typically significantly different from the characteristics of the asset classes themselves.

11. Which of Velky's statements about risk budgeting is correct?
     A. Statement 1
     B. Statement 2
     C. Statement 3

12. Which of Chaterji's criticisms of MVO is/are valid?
     A. Only Criticism 1
     B. Only Criticism 2
     C. Both Criticism 1 and Criticism 2

13. Which of the characteristics put forth by Chaterji to describe the factor-based approach is/are correct?
     A. Only Characteristic 1
     B. Only Characteristic 2
     C. Both Characteristic 1 and Characteristic 2

14. John Tomb is an investment advisor at an asset management firm. He is developing an asset allocation for James Youngmall, a client of the firm. Tomb considers two possible allocations for Youngmall. Allocation A consists of four asset classes: cash, US bonds, US equities, and global equities. Allocation B includes these same four asset classes, as well as global bonds. Youngmall has a relatively low risk tolerance with a risk aversion coefficient (λ) of 7. Tomb runs mean–variance optimization (MVO) to maximize the following utility function to determine the preferred allocation for Youngmall:

$$U_m = E(R_m) - 0.005\lambda\sigma_m^2$$

The resulting MVO statistics for the two asset allocations are presented in Exhibit 1.

EXHIBIT 1   MVO Portfolio Statistics

	Allocation A	Allocation B
Expected return	6.7%	5.9%
Expected standard deviation	11.9%	10.7%

     Determine which allocation in Exhibit 1 Tomb should recommend to Youngmall. **Justify** your response.

Determine which allocation in Exhibit 1 Tomb should recommend to Youngmall. (circle one)

Allocation A	Allocation B

     Justify your response.

15. Walker Patel is a portfolio manager at an investment management firm. After successfully implementing mean–variance optimization (MVO), he wants to apply reverse optimization to his portfolio. For each asset class in the portfolio, Patel obtains market capitalization data, betas computed relative to a global market portfolio, and

expected returns. This information, along with the MVO asset allocation results, are presented in Exhibit 1.

EXHIBIT 1   Asset Class Data and MVO Asset Allocation Results

Asset Class	Market Cap (trillions)	Beta	Expected Returns	MVO Asset Allocation
Cash	$4.2	0.0	2.0%	10%
US bonds	$26.8	0.5	4.5%	20%
US equities	$22.2	1.4	8.6%	35%
Global equities	$27.5	1.7	10.5%	20%
Global bonds	$27.1	0.6	4.7%	15%
Total	$107.8			

The risk-free rate is 2.0%, and the global market risk premium is 5.5%.

Contrast, using the information provided above, the results of a reverse optimization approach with that of the MVO approach for each of the following:

i.   The asset allocation mix

ii.   The values of the expected returns for US equities and global bonds

Justify your response.

16.   Viktoria Johansson is newly appointed as manager of ABC Corporation's pension fund. The current market value of the fund's assets is $10 billion, and the present value of the fund's liabilities is $8.5 billion. The fund has historically been managed using an asset-only approach, but Johansson recommends to ABC's board of directors that they adopt a liability-relative approach, specifically the hedging/return-seeking portfolios approach. Johansson assumes that the returns of the fund's liabilities are driven by changes in the returns of index-linked government bonds. Exhibit 1 presents three potential asset allocation choices for the fund.

EXHIBIT 1   Potential Asset Allocations Choices for ABC Corp's Pension Fund

Asset Class	Allocation 1	Allocation 2	Allocation 3
Cash	15%	5%	0%
Index-linked government bonds	70%	15%	85%
Corporate bonds	0%	30%	5%
Equities	15%	50%	10%
Portfolio Statistics			
Expected return	3.4%	6.2%	3.6%
Expected standard deviation	7.0%	12.0%	8.5%

Determine which asset allocation in Exhibit 1 would be *most appropriate* for Johansson given her recommendation. **Justify** your response.

Determine which asset allocation in Exhibit 1 would be *most appropriate* for Johansson given her recommendation.
(circle one)

Allocation 1	Allocation 2	Allocation 3

Justify your response.

The following information relates to Questions 17 and 18

Mike and Kerry Armstrong are a married couple who recently retired with total assets of $8 million. The Armstrongs meet with their financial advisor, Brent Abbott, to discuss three of their financial goals during their retirement.

Goal 1: An 85% chance of purchasing a vacation home for $5 million in five years.
Goal 2: A 99% chance of being able to maintain their current annual expenditures of $100,000 for the next 10 years, assuming annual inflation of 3% from Year 2 onward.
Goal 3: A 75% chance of being able to donate $10 million to charitable foundations in 25 years.

Abbott suggests using a goals-based approach to construct a portfolio. He develops a set of sub-portfolio modules, presented in Exhibit 1. Abbott suggests investing any excess capital in Module A.

EXHIBIT 1   "Highest Probability- and Horizon-Adjusted Return" Sub-Portfolio Modules under Different Horizon and Probability Scenarios

Portfolio Characteristics	A	B	C	D
Expected return	6.5%	7.9%	8.5%	8.8%
Expected volatility	6.0%	7.7%	8.8%	9.7%
Annualized Minimum Expectation Returns				
Time Horizon	5 Years			
Required Success				
99%	0.3%	–0.1%	–0.7%	–1.3%
85%	3.7%	4.3%	4.4%	4.3%
75%	4.7%	5.6%	5.8%	5.9%
Time Horizon	10 Years			
Required Success				
99%	2.1%	2.2%	2.0%	1.7%
85%	4.5%	5.4%	5.6%	5.6%
75%	5.2%	6.3%	6.6%	6.7%
Time Horizon	25 Years			

Required Success				
99%	3.7%	4.3%	4.4%	4.3%
85%	5.3%	6.3%	6.7%	6.8%
75%	5.7%	6.9%	7.3%	7.5%

17. **Select**, for each of Armstrong's three goals, which sub-portfolio module from Exhibit 1 Abbott should choose in constructing a portfolio. **Justify** each selection.

Select, for each of Armstrong's three goals, which sub-portfolio module from Exhibit 1 Abbott should choose in constructing a portfolio.
(circle one module for each goal)

Goal 1	Goal 2	Goal 3
Module A	Module A	Module A
Module B	Module B	Module B
Module C	Module C	Module C
Module D	Module D	Module D

Justify each selection.

18. **Construct** the overall goals-based asset allocation for the Armstrongs given their three goals and Abbott's suggestion for investing any excess capital. **Show** your calculations.

Construct the overall goals-based asset allocation for the Armstrongs given their three goals and Abbott's suggestion for investing any excess capital.
(insert the percentage of the total assets to be invested in each module)

Module A	Module B	Module C	Module D

Show your calculations.

CHAPTER 7

ASSET ALLOCATION WITH REAL-WORLD CONSTRAINTS

LEARNING OUTCOMES

The candidate should be able to:

- discuss asset size, liquidity needs, time horizon, and regulatory or other considerations as constraints on asset allocation;
- discuss tax considerations in asset allocation and rebalancing;
- recommend and justify revisions to an asset allocation given change(s) in investment objectives and/or constraints;
- discuss the use of short-term shifts in asset allocation;
- identify behavioral biases that arise in asset allocation and recommend methods to overcome them.

SUMMARY

- The primary constraints on an asset allocation decision are asset size, liquidity, time horizon, and other external considerations, such as taxes and regulation.
- The size of an asset owner's portfolio may limit the asset classes accessible to the asset owner. An asset owner's portfolio may be too small—or too large—to capture the returns of certain asset classes or strategies efficiently.
- Complex asset classes and investment vehicles require sufficient governance capacity.
- Large-scale asset owners may achieve operating efficiencies, but they may find it difficult to deploy capital effectively in certain active investment strategies given liquidity conditions and trading costs.
- Smaller portfolios may also be constrained by size. They may be too small to adequately diversify across the range of asset classes and investment managers, or they may have staffing constraints that prevent them from monitoring a complex investment program.

- Investors with smaller portfolios may be constrained in their ability to access private equity, private real estate, hedge funds, and infrastructure investments because of the high required minimum investments and regulatory restrictions associated with those asset classes. Wealthy families may pool assets to meet the required minimums.
- The liquidity needs of the asset owner and the liquidity characteristics of the asset classes each influence the available opportunity set.
- Liquidity needs must also take into consideration the financial strength of the investor and resources beyond those held in the investment portfolio.
- When assessing the appropriateness of any given asset class for a given investor, it is important to evaluate potential liquidity needs in the context of an extreme market stress event.
- An investor's time horizon must be considered in any asset allocation exercise. Changes in human capital and the changing character of liabilities are two important time-related constraints of asset allocation.
- External considerations—such as regulations, tax rules, funding, and financing needs—are also likely to influence the asset allocation decision.
- Taxes alter the distribution of returns by both reducing the expected mean return and muting the dispersion of returns. Asset values and asset risk and return inputs to asset allocation should be modified to reflect the tax status of the investor. Correlation assumptions do not need to be adjusted, but taxes do affect the return and the standard deviation assumptions for each asset class.
- Periodic portfolio rebalancing to return the portfolio to its target strategic asset allocation is an integral part of sound portfolio management. Taxable investors must consider the tax implications of rebalancing.
- Rebalancing thresholds may be wider for taxable portfolios because it takes larger asset class movements to materially alter the risk profile of the taxable portfolio.
- Strategic asset location is the placement of less tax-efficient assets in accounts with more-favorable tax treatment.
- An asset owner's strategic asset allocation should be re-examined periodically, even in the absence of a change in the asset owner's circumstances.
- A special review of the asset allocation policy may be triggered by a change in goals, constraints, or beliefs.
- In some situations, a change to an asset allocation strategy may be implemented without a formal asset allocation study. Anticipating key milestones that would alter the asset owner's risk appetite, and implementing pre-established changes to the asset allocation in response, is often referred to as a "glide path."
- Tactical asset allocation (TAA) allows short-term deviations from the strategic asset allocation (SAA) targets and are expected to increase risk-adjusted return. Using either short-term views or signals, the investor actively re-weights broad asset classes, sectors, or risk-factor premiums. The sizes of these deviations from the SAA are often constrained by the Investment Policy Statement.
- The success of TAA decisions is measured against the performance of the SAA policy portfolio by comparing Sharpe ratios, evaluating the information ratio or the t-statistic of the average excess return of the TAA portfolio relative to the SAA portfolio, or plotting outcomes versus the efficient frontier.
- TAA incurs trading and tax costs. Tactical trades can also increase the concentration of risk.

- Discretionary TAA relies on a qualitative interpretation of political, economic, and financial market conditions and is predicated on a belief of persistent manager skill in predicting and timing short-term market moves.
- Systematic TAA relies on quantitative signals to capture documented return anomalies that may be inconsistent with market efficiency.
- The behavioral biases most relevant in asset allocation include loss aversion, the illusion of control, mental accounting, recency bias, framing, and availability bias.
- An effective investment program will address behavioral biases through a formal asset allocation process with its own objective framework, governance, and controls.
- In goals-based investing, loss-aversion bias can be mitigated by framing risk in terms of shortfall probability or by funding high-priority goals with low-risk assets.
- The cognitive bias, illusion of control, and hindsight bias can all be mitigated by using a formal asset allocation process that uses long-term return and risk forecasts, optimization constraints anchored around asset class weights in the global market portfolio, and strict policy ranges.
- Goals-based investing incorporates the mental accounting bias directly into the asset allocation solution by aligning each goal with a discrete sub-portfolio.
- A formal asset allocation policy with pre-specified allowable ranges may constrain recency bias.
- The framing bias effect can be mitigated by presenting the possible asset allocation choices with multiple perspectives on the risk/reward trade-off.
- Familiarity bias, a form of availability bias, most commonly results in an overweight in home country securities and may also cause investors to inappropriately compare their investment decisions (and performance) to other organizations. Familiarity bias can be mitigated by using the global market portfolio as the starting point in developing the asset allocation and by carefully evaluating any potential deviations from this baseline portfolio.
- A strong governance framework with the appropriate level of expertise and well-documented investment beliefs increases the likelihood that shifts in asset allocation are made objectively and in accordance with those beliefs. This will help to mitigate the effect that behavioral biases may have on the long-term success of the investment program.

PRACTICE PROBLEMS

The following information relates to questions 1–6

Rebecca Mayer is an asset management consultant for institutions and high-net-worth individuals. Mayer meets with Sebastian Capara, the newly appointed Investment Committee chairman for the Kinkardeen University Endowment (KUE), a very large tax-exempt fund.

Capara and Mayer review KUE's current and strategic asset allocations, which are presented in Exhibit 1. Capara informs Mayer that over the last few years, Kinkardeen University has financed its operations primarily from tuition, with minimal need of financial support from KUE. Enrollment at the University has been rising in recent years, and the Board of Trustees expects enrollment growth to continue for the next five years. Consequently, the board expects very modest endowment support to be needed during that time. These expectations led the Investment Committee to approve a decrease in the endowment's annual spending rate starting in the next fiscal year.

EXHIBIT 1   Kinkardeen University Endowment—Strategic Asset Allocation Policy

Asset Class	Current Weight	Target Allocation	Lower Policy Limit	Upper Policy Limit
Developed markets equity	30%	30%	25%	35%
Emerging markets equity	28%	30%	25%	35%
Investment-grade bonds	15%	20%	15%	25%
Private real estate equity	15%	10%	5%	15%
Infrastructure	12%	10%	5%	15%

As an additional source of alpha, Mayer proposes tactically adjusting KUE's asset-class weights to profit from short-term return opportunities. To confirm his understanding of tactical asset allocation (TAA), Capara tells Mayer the following:

Statement 1.   The Sharpe ratio is suitable for measuring the success of TAA relative to SAA.
Statement 2.   Discretionary TAA attempts to capture asset-class-level return anomalies that have been shown to have some predictability and persistence.
Statement 3.   TAA allows a manager to deviate from the IPS asset-class upper and lower limits if the shift is expected to produce higher expected risk-adjusted returns.

Capara asks Mayer to recommend a TAA strategy based on excess return forecasts for the asset classes in KUE's portfolio, as shown in Exhibit 2.

EXHIBIT 2   Short-Term Excess Return Forecast

Asset Class	Expected Excess Return
Developed markets equity	2%
Emerging markets equity	5%
Investment-grade bonds	–3%
Private real estate equity	3%
Infrastructure	–1%

Following her consultation with Capara, Mayer meets with Roger Koval, a member of a wealthy family. Although Koval's baseline needs are secured by a family trust, Koval has a personal portfolio to fund his lifestyle goals.

In Koval's country, interest income is taxed at progressively higher income tax rates. Dividend income and long-term capital gains are taxed at lower tax rates relative to interest and earned income. In taxable accounts, realized capital losses can be used to offset current or future realized capital gains. Koval is in a high tax bracket, and his taxable account currently holds, in equal weights, high-yield bonds, investment-grade bonds, and domestic equities focused on long-term capital gains.

Koval asks Mayer about adding new asset classes to the taxable portfolio. Mayer suggests emerging markets equity given its positive short-term excess return forecast. However, Koval tells Mayer he is not interested in adding emerging markets equity to the account because he is convinced it is too risky. Koval justifies this belief by referring to significant losses the family trust suffered during the recent economic crisis.

Mayer also suggests using two mean–variance portfolio optimization scenarios for the taxable account to evaluate potential asset allocations. Mayer recommends running two optimizations: one on a pre-tax basis and another on an after-tax basis.

1. The change in the annual spending rate, in conjunction with the board's expectations regarding future enrollment and the need for endowment support, could justify that KUE's target weight for:
   A. infrastructure be increased.
   B. investment-grade bonds be increased.
   C. private real estate equity be decreased.

2. Which of Capara's statements regarding tactical asset allocation is correct?
   A. Statement 1
   B. Statement 2
   C. Statement 3

3. Based on Exhibits 1 and 2, to attempt to profit from the short-term excess return forecast, Capara should increase KUE's portfolio allocation to:
   A. developed markets equity and decrease its allocation to infrastructure.
   B. emerging markets equity and decrease its allocation to investment-grade bonds.
   C. developed markets equity and increase its allocation to private real estate equity.

4. Given Koval's current portfolio and the tax laws of the country in which he lives, Koval's portfolio would be more tax efficient if he reallocated his taxable account to hold more:
   A. high-yield bonds.
   B. investment-grade bonds.
   C. domestic equities focused on long-term capital gain opportunities.

5. Koval's attitude toward emerging markets equity reflects which of the following behavioral biases?
   A. Hindsight bias
   B. Availability bias
   C. Illusion of control

6. In both of Mayer's optimization scenarios, which of the following model inputs could be used without adjustment?
   A. Expected returns
   B. Correlation of returns
   C. Standard deviations of returns

The following information relates to questions 7–13

Elsbeth Quinn and Dean McCall are partners at Camel Asset Management (CAM). Quinn advises high-net-worth individuals, and McCall specializes in retirement plans for institutions.

Quinn meets with Neal and Karina Martin, both age 44. The Martins plan to retire at age 62. Twenty percent of the Martins' $600,000 in financial assets is held in cash and earmarked for funding their daughter Lara's university studies, which begin in one year. Lara's education and their own retirement are the Martins' highest-priority goals. Last week, the Martins learned that Lara was awarded a four-year full scholarship for university. Quinn reviews how the scholarship might affect the Martins' asset allocation strategy.

The Martins have assets in both taxable and tax-deferred accounts. For baseline retirement needs, Quinn recommends that the Martins maintain their current overall 60% equity/40% bonds (± 8% rebalancing range) strategic asset allocation. Quinn calculates that given current financial assets and expected future earnings, the Martins could reduce future retirement savings by 15% and still comfortably retire at 62. The Martins wish to allocate that 15% to a sub-portfolio with the goal of making a charitable gift to their alma mater from their estate. Although the gift is a low-priority goal, the Martins want the sub-portfolio to earn the highest return possible. Quinn promises to recommend an asset allocation strategy for the Martins' aspirational goal.

Next, Quinn discusses taxation of investments with the Martins. Their interest income is taxed at 35%, and capital gains and dividends are taxed at 20%. The Martins want to minimize taxes. Based on personal research, Neal makes the following two statements:

Statement 1.   The after-tax return volatility of assets held in taxable accounts will be less than the pre-tax return volatility.
Statement 2.   Assets that receive more favorable tax treatment should be held in tax-deferred accounts.

The equity portion of the Martins' portfolios produced an annualized return of 20% for the past three years. As a result, the Martins' equity allocation in both their taxable and tax-deferred portfolios has increased to 71%, with bonds falling to 29%. The Martins want to keep the strategic asset allocation risk levels the same in both types of retirement portfolios. Quinn discusses rebalancing; however, Neal is somewhat reluctant to take money out of stocks, expressing confidence that strong investment returns will continue.

Quinn's CAM associate, McCall, meets with Bruno Snead, the director of the Katt Company Pension Fund (KCPF). The strategic asset allocation for the fund is 65% stocks/ 35% bonds. Because of favorable returns during the past eight recession-free years, the KCPF is now overfunded. However, there are early signs of the economy weakening. Since Katt Company is in a cyclical industry, the Pension Committee is concerned about future market and economic risk and fears that the high-priority goal of maintaining a fully funded status may be adversely affected. McCall suggests to Snead that the KCPF might benefit from an updated IPS. Following a thorough review, McCall recommends a new IPS and strategic asset allocation.

The proposed IPS revisions include a plan for short-term deviations from strategic asset allocation targets. The goal is to benefit from equity market trends by automatically increasing (decreasing) the allocation to equities by 5% whenever the S&P 500 Index 50-day moving average crosses above (below) the 200-day moving average.

7. Given the change in funding of Lara's education, the Martins' strategic asset allocation would *most likely* decrease exposure to:
   A. cash.
   B. bonds.
   C. equities.

8. The *most appropriate* asset allocation for the Martins' new charitable gift sub-portfolio is:
   A. 40% equities/60% bonds.
   B. 70% equities/30% bonds.
   C. 100% equities/0% bonds.

9. Which of Neal's statements regarding the taxation of investments is correct?
   A. Statement 1 only
   B. Statement 2 only
   C. Both Statement 1 and Statement 2

10. Given the Martins' risk and tax preferences, the taxable portfolio should be rebalanced:
    A. less often than the tax-deferred portfolio.
    B. as often as the tax-deferred portfolio.
    C. more often than the tax-deferred portfolio.

11. During the rebalancing discussion, which behavioral bias does Neal exhibit?
    A. Framing bias
    B. Loss aversion
    C. Representativeness bias

12. Given McCall's IPS recommendation, the *most appropriate* new strategic asset allocation for the KCPF is:
    A. 40% stocks/60% bonds.
    B. 65% stocks/35% bonds.
    C. 75% stocks/25% bonds.

13. The proposal for short-term adjustments to the KCPF asset allocation strategy is known as:
    A. de-risking.
    B. systematic tactical asset allocation.
    C. discretionary tactical asset allocation.

The following information relates to questions 14–18

Emma Young, a 47-year-old single mother of two daughters, ages 7 and 10, recently sold a business for $5.5 million net of taxes and put the proceeds into a money market account. Her other assets include a tax-deferred retirement account worth $3.0 million, a $500,000 after-tax account designated for her daughters' education, a $400,000 after-tax account for unexpected needs, and her home, which she owns outright.

Her living expenses are fully covered by her job. Young wants to retire in 15 years and to fund her retirement from existing assets. An orphan at eight who experienced childhood financial hardships, she places a high priority on retirement security and wants to avoid losing money in any of her three accounts.

14. **Identify** the behavioral biases Young is *most likely* exhibiting.

    Justify each response.

Identify the behavioral biases Young is *most likely* exhibiting. (Circle the correct answers.)

Justify each response.

Bias	Justification
Loss Aversion	
Illusion of Control	
Mental Accounting	
Representative Bias	
Framing Bias	
Availability Bias	

    A broker proposes to Young three portfolios, shown in Exhibit 1. The broker also provides Young with asset class estimated returns and portfolio standard deviations in Exhibit 2 and Exhibit 3, respectively. The broker notes that there is a $500,000 minimum investment requirement for alternative assets. Finally, because the funds in the money market account are readily investible, the broker suggests using that account only for this initial investment round.

EXHIBIT 1   Proposed Portfolios

Asset Class	Portfolio 1	Portfolio 2	Portfolio 3
Municipal Bonds	5%	35%	30%
Small-Cap Equities	50%	10%	35%
Large-Cap Equities	35%	50%	35%
Private Equity	10%	5%	0%
Total	100%	100%	100%

EXHIBIT 2   Asset Class Pre-Tax Returns

Asset Class	Pre-Tax Return
Municipal Bonds	3%
Small-Cap Equities	12%
Large-Cap Equities	10%
Private Equity	25%

EXHIBIT 3   Portfolio Standard Deviations

Proposed Portfolio	Post-Tax Standard Deviation
Portfolio 1	28.2%
Portfolio 2	16.3%
Portfolio 3	15.5%

Young wants to earn at least 6.0% after tax per year, without taking on additional incremental risk. Young's capital gains and overall tax rate is 25%.

15. **Determine** which proposed portfolio *most closely* meets Young's desired objectives. **Justify** your response.

Determine which proposed portfolio *most closely* meets Young's desired objectives. (Circle one.)

Portfolio 1	Portfolio 2	Portfolio 3

Justify your response.

The broker suggests that Young rebalance her $5.5 million money market account and the $3.0 million tax-deferred retirement account periodically in order to maintain their targeted allocations. The broker proposes the same risk profile for the equity positions with two potential target equity allocations and rebalancing ranges for the two accounts as follows:

- Alternative 1: 80% equities +/– 8.0% rebalancing range
- Alternative 2: 75% equities +/– 10.7% rebalancing range

16. **Determine** which alternative *best* fits each account. **Justify** each selection.

Determine which alternative (circle one) *best* fits each account.

Account	Alternative	Justify each selection.
$5.5 Million Account	Alternative 1 Alternative 2	
$3.0 Million Account	Alternative 1 Alternative 2	

Ten years later, Young is considering an early-retirement package offer. The package would provide continuing salary and benefits for three years. The broker recommends a special review of Young's financial plan to assess potential changes to the existing allocation strategy.

17. **Identify** the *primary* reason for the broker's reassessment of Young's circumstances. **Justify** your response.

Identify the *primary* reason for the broker's reassessment of Young's circumstances. (Circle one.)

Change in goals	Change in constraints	Change in beliefs

Justify your response.

Young decides to accept the retirement offer. Having very low liquidity needs, she wants to save part of the retirement payout for unforeseen costs that might occur more than a decade in the future. The broker's view on long-term stock market prospects is positive and recommends additional equity investment.

18. **Determine** which of Young's accounts (education, retirement, reallocated money market, or unexpected needs) is *best* suited for implementing the broker's recommendation.

Determine which of Young's accounts is *best* suited for implementing the broker's recommendation. (Circle one.)

Account	Justification
Education	
Reallocated Money Market	
Retirement	
Unexpected Needs	

The following information relates to questions 19–20

Mark DuBord, a financial adviser, works with two university foundations, the Titan State Foundation (Titan) and the Fordhart University Foundation (Fordhart). He meets with each university foundation investment committee annually to review fund objectives and constraints.

Titan's portfolio has a market value of $10 million. After his annual meeting with its investment committee, DuBord notes the following points:

- Titan must spend 3% of its beginning-of-the-year asset value annually to meet legal obligations.
- The investment committee seeks exposure to private equity investments and requests DuBord's review of the Sun-Fin Private Equity Fund as a potential new investment.

- A recent declining trend in enrollment is expected to continue. This is a concern because it has led to a loss of operating revenue from tuition.
- Regulatory sanctions and penalties are likely to result in lower donations over the next five years.

DuBord supervises two junior analysts and instructs one to formulate new allocations for Titan. This analyst proposes the allocation presented in Exhibit 1.

EXHIBIT 1   Fund Information for Titan

Fund Name	Existing Allocation	Proposed Allocation	Fund Size in Billions (AUM)	Fund Minimum Investment
Global Equity Fund	70%	70%	$25	$500,000
Investment-Grade Bond Fund	27%	17%	$50	$250,000
Sun-Fin Private Equity Fund	0%	10%	$0.40	$1,000,000
Cash Equivalent Fund	3%	3%	$50	$100,000

19. **Discuss** *two* reasons why the proposed asset allocation is inappropriate for Titan.

The Fordhart portfolio has a market value of $2 billion. After his annual meeting with its investment committee, DuBord notes the following points:

- Fordhart must spend 3% of its beginning-of-the-year asset value annually to meet legal obligations.
- The investment committee seeks exposure to private equity investments and requests that DuBord review the CFQ Private Equity Fund as a potential new investment.
- Enrollment is strong and growing, leading to increased operating revenues from tuition.
- A recent legal settlement eliminated an annual obligation of $50 million from the portfolio to support a biodigester used in the university's Center for Renewable Energy.

DuBord instructs his second junior analyst to formulate new allocations for Fordhart. This analyst proposes the allocation presented in Exhibit 2.

EXHIBIT 2   Fund Information for Fordhart

Fund Name	Existing Allocation	Proposed Allocation	Fund Size in Billions (AUM)	Fund Minimum Investment
Large-Cap Equity Fund	49%	29%	$50	$250,000
Investment-Grade Bond Fund	49%	59%	$80	$500,000
CFQ Private Equity Fund	0%	10%	$0.5	$5,000,000
Cash Equivalent Fund	2%	2%	$50	$250,000

20. **Discuss** *two* reasons why the proposed asset allocation is inappropriate for Fordhart.

CHAPTER 8

ASSET ALLOCATION TO ALTERNATIVE INVESTMENTS

LEARNING OUTCOMES

The candidate should be able to:

- explain the roles that alternative investments play in multi-asset portfolios;
- compare alternative investments and bonds as risk mitigators in relation to a long equity position;
- compare traditional and risk-based approaches to defining the investment opportunity set, including alternative investments;
- discuss investment considerations that are important in allocating to different types of alternative investments;
- discuss suitability considerations in allocating to alternative investments;
- discuss approaches to asset allocation to alternative investments;
- discuss the importance of liquidity planning in allocating to alternative investments;
- discuss considerations in monitoring alternative investment programs.

SUMMARY

- Allocations to alternatives are believed to increase a portfolio's risk-adjusted return. An investment in alternatives typically fulfills one or more of four roles in an investor's portfolio: capital growth, income generation, risk diversification, and/or safety.
- Private equity investments are generally viewed as return enhancers in a portfolio of traditional assets.

- Long/short equity strategies are generally believed to deliver equity-like returns with less than full exposure to the equity premium. Short-biased equity strategies are expected to lower a portfolio's overall equity beta while producing some measure of alpha. Arbitrage and event-driven strategies are expected to provide equity-like returns with little to no correlation with traditional asset classes.
- Real assets (e.g., commodities, farmland, timber, energy, and infrastructure assets) are generally perceived to provide a hedge against inflation.
- Timber investments provide both growth and inflation-hedging properties.
- Commodities (e.g., metals, energy, livestock, and agricultural commodities) serve as a hedge against inflation and provide a differentiated source of alpha. Certain commodity investments serve as safe havens in times of crisis.
- Farmland investing may have a commodity-like profile or a commercial real-estate-like profile.
- Energy investments are generally considered a real asset as the investor owns the mineral rights to commodities that are correlated with inflation factors.
- Infrastructure investments tend to generate stable/modestly growing income and to have high correlation with overall inflation.
- Real estate strategies range from core to opportunistic and are believed to provide protection against unanticipated increases in inflation. Core real estate strategies are more income-oriented, while opportunistic strategies rely more heavily on capital appreciation.
- Bonds have been a more effective volatility mitigator than alternatives over shorter time horizons.
- The traditional approaches to defining asset classes are easy to communicate and implement. However, they tend to over-estimate portfolio diversification and obscure primary drivers of risk.
- Typical risk factors applied to alternative investments include equity, size, value, liquidity, duration, inflation, credit spread, and currency. A benefit of the risk factor approach is that every asset class can be described using the same framework.
- Risk factor-based approaches have certain limitations. A framework with too many factors is difficult to administer and interpret, but too small a set of risk factors may not accurately describe the characteristics of alternative asset classes. Risk factor sensitivities are highly sensitive to the historical look-back period.
- Investors with less than a 15-year investment horizon should generally avoid investments in private real estate, private real asset, and private equity funds.
- Investors must consider whether they have the necessary skills, expertise, and resources to build an alternative investment program internally. Investors without a strong governance program are less likely to develop a successful alternative investment program.
- Reporting for alternative funds is often less transparent than investors are accustomed to seeing on their stock and bond portfolios. For many illiquid strategies, reporting is often received well past typical monthly or quarter-end deadlines. Full, position-level transparency is rare in many alternative strategies.
- Three primary approaches are used to determine the desired allocation to the alternative asset classes:
  - Monte Carlo simulation may be used to generate return scenarios that relax the assumption of normally distributed returns.
  - Optimization techniques, which incorporate downside risk or take into account skew, may be used to enhance the asset allocation process.

- Risk factor-based approaches to alternative asset allocation can be applied to develop more robust asset allocation proposals.
- Two key analytical challenges in modeling allocations to alternatives include stale and/or artificially smoothed returns and return distributions that exhibit significant skewness and fat tails (or excess kurtosis).
- Artificially smoothed returns can be detected by testing the return stream for serial correlation. The analyst needs to unsmooth the returns to get a more accurate representation of the risk and return characteristics of the asset class.
- Skewness and kurtosis can be dealt with by using empirically observed asset returns because they incorporate the actual distribution. Advanced mathematical or statistical models can also be used to capture the true behavior of alternative asset classes.
- Applications of Monte Carlo simulation in allocating to alternative investments include:
  1. simulating skewed and fat-tailed financial variables by estimating the behavior of factors and/or assets in low-volatility regimes and high-volatility regimes, then generating scenarios using the different means and covariances estimated under the different regimes; and
  2. simulating portfolio outcomes ($+/-$ 1 standard deviation) to estimate the likelihood of falling short of the investment objectives.
- Unconstrained mean–variance optimization (MVO) often leads to portfolios dominated by cash and fixed income at the low-risk end of the spectrum and by private equity at the high-risk end of the spectrum. Some investors impose minimum and maximum constraints on asset classes. Slight changes in the input variables could lead to substantial changes in the asset allocations.
- Mean–CVaR optimization may be used to identify allocations that minimize downside risk rather than simply volatility.
- Investors may choose to optimize allocations to risk factors rather than asset classes. These allocations, however, must be implemented using asset classes. Portfolios with similar risk factor exposures can have vastly different asset allocations.
- Some caveats with respect to risk factor-based allocations are that investors may hold different definitions for a given risk factor, correlations among risk factors may shift under changing market conditions, and some factor sensitivities are very unstable.
- Cash flow and commitment-pacing models enable investors in private alternatives to better manage their portfolio liquidity and set realistic annual commitment targets to reach the desired asset allocation.
- An alternative investment program should be monitored relative to the goals established for the alternative investment program, not simply relative to a benchmark. The investor must monitor developments in the relevant markets to ensure that the fundamental thesis underlying the decision to invest remains intact.
- Two common benchmarking approaches to benchmarking alternative investments—custom index proxies and peer group comparisons—have significant limitations.
- IRRs are sensitive to the timing of cash flows into and out of the fund: Two managers may have similar portfolios but different return profiles depending on their capital call and distribution schedule.
- Pricing issues can distort reported returns and the associated risk metrics, such as betas, correlations, and Sharpe ratios.
- Monitoring of the firm and the investment process are particularly important in alternative investment structures where the manager cannot be terminated easily. Key elements to

monitor include key person risk, alignment of interests, style drift, risk management, client/asset turnover, client profile, and service providers.

PRACTICE PROBLEMS

The following information relates to Questions 1–8

Kevin Kroll is the chair of the investment committee responsible for the governance of the Shire Manufacturing Corporation (SMC) defined benefit pension plan. The pension fund is currently fully funded and has followed an asset mix of 60% public equities and 40% bonds since Kroll has been chair. Kroll meets with Mary Park, an actuarial and pension consultant, to discuss issues raised at the last committee meeting.

Kroll notes that the investment committee would like to explore the benefits of adding alternative investments to the pension plan's strategic asset allocation. Kroll states:

Statement 1: The committee would like to know which alternative asset would best mitigate the risks to the portfolio due to unexpected inflation and also have a relatively low correlation with public equities to provide diversification benefits.

The SMC pension plan has been able to fund the annual pension payments without any corporate contributions for a number of years. The committee is interested in potential changes to the asset mix that could increase the probability of achieving the long-term investment target return of 5.5% while maintaining the funded status of the plan. Park notes that fixed-income yields are expected to remain low for the foreseeable future. Kroll asks:

Statement 2: If the public equity allocation remains at 60%, is there a single asset class that could be used for the balance of the portfolio to achieve the greatest probability of maintaining the pension funding status over a long time horizon? Under this hypothetical scenario, the balance of the portfolio can be allocated to either bonds, hedge funds, or private equities.

Park confirms with Kroll that the committee has historically used a traditional approach to define the opportunity set based on distinct macroeconomic regimes, and she proposes that a risk-based approach might be a better method. Although the traditional approach is relatively powerful for its ability to handle liquidity and manager selection issues compared to a risk-based approach, they both acknowledge that a number of limitations are associated with the existing approach.

Park presents a report (Exhibit 1) that proposes a new strategic asset allocation for the pension plan. Kroll states that one of the concerns that the investment committee will have regarding the new allocation is that the pension fund needs to be able to fund an upcoming early retirement incentive program (ERIP) that SMC will be offering to its employees within the next two years. Employees who have reached the age of 55 and whose age added to the number of years of company service sum to 75 or more can retire 10 years early and receive the defined benefit pension normally payable at age 65.

EXHIBIT 1   Proposed Asset Allocation of SMC Defined Benefit Pension Plan

Asset Class	Public Equities	Broad Fixed Income	Private Equities	Hedge Funds	Public Real Estate	Total
Target	45%	25%	10%	10%	10%	100%
Range	35%–55%	15%–35%	0%–12%	0%–12%	0%–12%	–

Kroll and Park then discuss suitability considerations related to the allocation in Exhibit 1. Kroll understands that one of the drawbacks of including the proposed alternative asset classes is that daily reporting will no longer be available. Investment reports for alternatives will likely be received after monthly or quarter-end deadlines used for the plan's traditional investments. Park emphasizes that in a typical private equity structure, the pension fund makes a commitment of capital to a blind pool as part of the private investment partnership.

In order to explain the new strategic asset allocation to the investment committee, Kroll asks Park why a risk factor-based approach should be used rather than a mean–variance-optimization technique. Park makes the following statements:

Statement 3:   Risk factor-based approaches to asset allocation produce more robust asset allocation proposals.

Statement 4:   A mean–variance optimization typically overallocates to the private alternative asset classes due to stale pricing.

Park notes that the current macroeconomic environment could lead to a bear market within a few years. Kroll asks Park to discuss the potential impact on liquidity planning associated with the actions of the fund's general partners in the forecasted environment.

Kroll concludes the meeting by reviewing the information in Exhibit 2 pertaining to three potential private equity funds analyzed by Park. Park discloses the following due diligence findings from a recent manager search: Fund A retains administrators, custodians, and auditors with impeccable reputations; Fund B has achieved its performance in a manner that appears to conflict with its reported investment philosophy; and Fund C has recently experienced the loss of three key persons.

EXHIBIT 2   Potential Private Equity Funds, Internal Rate of Return (IRR)

Private Equity Fund	Fund A	Fund B	Fund C
5-year IRR	12.9%	13.2%	13.1%

1. Based on Statement 1, Park should recommend:
    A. hedge funds.
    B. private equities.
    C. commodity futures.

2. In answering the question raised in Statement 2, Park would *most likely* recommend:
    A. bonds.
    B. hedge funds.
    C. private equities.

3. A limitation of the existing approach used by the committee to define the opportunity set is that it:
   A. is difficult to communicate.
   B. overestimates the portfolio diversification.
   C. is sensitive to the historical look-back period.

4. Based on Exhibit 1 and the proposed asset allocation, the greatest risk associated with the ERIP is:
   A. liability.
   B. leverage.
   C. liquidity.

5. The suitability concern discussed by Kroll and Park *most likely* deals with:
   A. governance.
   B. transparency.
   C. investment horizon.

6. Which of Park's statements regarding the asset allocation approaches is correct?
   A. Only Statement 3
   B. Only Statement 4
   C. Both Statement 3 and Statement 4

7. Based on the forecasted environment, liquidity planning should take into account that general partners may:
   A. call capital at a slower pace.
   B. make distributions at a faster pace.
   C. exercise an option to extend the life of the fund.

8. Based on Exhibit 2 and Park's due diligence, the pension committee should consider investing in:
   A. Fund A.
   B. Fund B.
   C. Fund C.

The following information relates to Questions 9–13

Eileen Gension is a portfolio manager for Zen-Alt Investment Consultants (Zen-Alt), which assists institutional investors with investing in alternative investments. Charles Smittand is an analyst at Zen-Alt and reports to Gension. Gension and Smittand discuss a new client, the Benziger University Endowment Fund (the fund), as well as a prospective client, the Opeptaja Pension Plan (the plan).

The fund's current portfolio is invested primarily in public equities, with the remainder invested in fixed income. The fund's investment objective is to support a 6% annual spending rate and to preserve the purchasing power of the asset base over a 10-year time horizon. The fund also wants to invest in assets that provide the highest amount of diversification against its dominant equity risk. Gension considers potential alternative investment options that would best meet the fund's diversification strategy.

In preparation for the first meeting between Zen-Alt and the fund, Gension and Smittand discuss implementing a short-biased equity strategy within the fund. Smittand makes the following three statements regarding short-biased equity strategies:

Statement 1:   Short-biased equity strategies generally provide alpha when used to diversify public equities.

Statement 2:   Short-biased equity strategies are expected to provide a higher reduction in volatility than bonds over a long time horizon.

Statement 3:   Short-biased equity strategies are expected to mitigate the risk of public equities by reducing the overall portfolio beta of the fund.

Gension directs Smittand to prepare asset allocation and portfolio characteristics data on three alternative portfolios. The fund's risk profile is one factor that potential lenders consider when assigning a risk rating to the university. A loan covenant with the university's primary lender states that a re-evaluation of the university's creditworthiness is triggered if the fund incurs a loss greater than 20% over any one-year period. Smittand states that the recommended asset allocation should achieve the following three goals, in order of priority and importance:

- Minimize the probability of triggering the primary lender's loan covenant.
- Minimize the probability of purchasing power impairment over a 10-year horizon.
- Maximize the probability of achieving a real return target of 6% over a 10-year horizon.

Smittand provides data for three alternative portfolios, which are presented in Exhibits 1 and 2.

EXHIBIT 1   Asset Allocation

Alternative Portfolio	Cash	Public Equity	Gov't.	Credit	Hedge Fund	Real Estate	Private Equity
A	4.0%	35.0%	6.0%	5.0%	20.0%	10.0%	20.0%
B	2.0%	40.0%	8.0%	3.0%	15.0%	7.0%	25.0%
C	1.0%	50.0%	3.0%	6.0%	10.0%	0.0%	30.0%

EXHIBIT 2   Portfolio Characteristics

Alternative Portfolio	1-Year 99% VaR	1-Year 99% CVaR	Probability of Meeting 6% Real Return (10-Year Horizon)	Probability of Purchasing Power Impairment (10-Year Horizon)
A	−16.3%	−19.4%	56.1%	2.5%
B	−17.4%	−20.6%	58.8%	2.8%
C	−19.3%	−22.7%	61.0%	4.0%

Notes:

- One-year horizon 99% VaR: the lowest return over any one-year period at a 99% confidence level
- One-year horizon 99% CVaR: the expected return if the return falls below the 99% VaR threshold
- Probability of purchasing power impairment: the probability of losing 40% of the fund's purchasing power over 10 years, after consideration of new gifts received by the fund, spending from the fund, and total returns

Gension next meets with the investment committee (IC) of the Opeptaja Pension Plan to discuss new opportunities in alternative investments. The plan is a $1 billion public pension fund that is required to provide detailed reports to the public and operates under specific government guidelines. The plan's IC adopted a formal investment policy that specifies an investment horizon of 20 years. The plan has a team of in-house analysts with significant experience in alternative investments.

During the meeting, the IC indicates that it is interested in investing in private real estate. Gension recommends a real estate investment managed by an experienced team with a proven track record. The investment will require multiple capital calls over the next few years. The IC proceeds to commit to the new real estate investment and seeks advice on liquidity planning related to the future capital calls.

9. Which asset class would *best* satisfy the Fund's diversification strategy?
   A. Private equity
   B. Private real estate
   C. Absolute return hedge fund

10. Which of Smittand's statements regarding short-biased equity strategies is *incorrect*?
    A. Statement 1
    B. Statement 2
    C. Statement 3

11. Based on Exhibit 2, which alternative portfolio should Gension recommend for the fund given Smittand's stated three goals?
    A. Portfolio A
    B. Portfolio B
    C. Portfolio C

12. Which of the following investor characteristics would *most likely* be a primary concern for the plan's IC with respect to investing in alternatives?
    A. Governance
    B. Transparency
    C. Investment horizon

13. With respect to liquidity planning relating to the plan's new real estate investment, Gension should recommend that the fund set aside appropriate funds and invest them in:
    A. 100% REITs.
    B. 100% cash equivalents.
    C. 80% cash equivalents and 20% REITs.

The following information relates to Questions 14–15

Ingerðria Greslö is an adviser with an investment management company and focuses on asset allocation for the company's high-net-worth investors. She prepares for a meeting with Maarten Pua, a new client who recently inherited a $10 million portfolio solely comprising public equities.

Greslö meets with Pua and proposes that she create a multi-asset portfolio by selling a portion of his equity holdings and investing the proceeds in another asset class. Greslö advises Pua that his investment objective should be to select an asset class that has a high potential to fulfill two functional roles: risk diversification and capital growth. Greslö suggests the following three asset classes:

- Public real estate
- Private real assets (timber)
- Equity long/short hedge funds

14. **Determine** which asset class is *most likely* to meet Pua's investment objective. **Justify** your response.

Determine which asset class is *most likely* to meet Pua's investment objective. (Circle one.)	**Justify** your response.
Public Real Estate	
Private Real Assets (Timber)	
Equity Long/Short Hedge Funds	

Five years after his first meeting with Pua, Greslö monitors a private real estate investment that Pua has held for one year. Until recently, the investment had been managed by a local real estate specialist who had a competitive advantage in this market; the specialist's strategy was to purchase distressed local residential housing properties, make strategic property improvements, and then sell them. Pua is one of several clients who have invested in this opportunity.

Greslö learns that the specialist recently retired and the investment is now managed by a national real estate company. The company has told investors that it now plans to invest throughout the region in both distressed housing and commercial properties. The company also lengthened the holding period for each investment property from the date of the initial capital call because of the complexity of the property renovations, and it altered the interim profit distribution targets.

15. **Discuss** the qualitative risk issues that have *most likely* materialized over the past year.

The following information relates to Questions 16–18

The Ælfheah Group is a US-based company with a relatively small pension plan. Ælfheah's investment committee (IC), whose members collectively have a relatively basic understanding of the investment process, has agreed that Ælfheah is willing to accept modest returns while the IC gains a better understanding of the process. Two key investment considerations for the IC are maintaining low overhead costs and minimizing taxes in the portfolio. Ælfheah has not been willing to incur the costs of in-house investment resources.

Qauhtèmoc Ng is the investment adviser for Ælfheah. He discusses with the IC its goal of diversifying Ælfheah's portfolio to include alternative assets. Ng suggests considering the following potential investment vehicles:

- Publicly traded US REIT
- Relative value hedge fund
- Tax-efficient angel investment

Ng explains that for the relative value hedge fund alternative, Ælfheah would be investing alongside tax-exempt investors.

16. **Determine** which of the potential investment vehicles *best* meets the investment considerations for Ælfheah. **Justify** your response. **Explain** for *each* investment not selected why the investment considerations are not met.

Determine which of the potential investment vehicles *best* meets the investment considerations for Ælfheah. (Circle one.)	**Justify** your response.	**Explain** for *each* investment not selected why the investment considerations are not met.
Publicly traded US REIT		
Relative value hedge fund		
Tax-efficient angel investment		

Ng and the IC review the optimal approach to determine the asset allocation for Ælfheah, including the traditional and risk-based approaches to defining the investment opportunity set.

17. **Determine** which approach to determine the asset allocation is *most appropriate* for Ælfheah. **Justify** your response.

Determine which approach to determine the asset allocation is *most appropriate* for Ælfheah. (Circle one.)	**Justify** your response.
Traditional	
Risk based	

The following year, Ng and the IC review the portfolio's performance. The IC has gained a better understanding of the investment process. The portfolio is meeting Ælfheah's liquidity needs, and Ng suggests that Ælfheah would benefit from diversifying into an additional alternative asset class. After discussing suitable investment vehicles for the proposed alternative asset class, Ng proposes the following three investment vehicles for further review:

- Funds of funds (FOFs)
- Separately managed accounts (SMAs)
- Undertakings for collective investment in transferable securities (UCITS)

18. **Determine** the investment vehicle that would be *most appropriate* for Ælfheah's proposed alternative asset class. **Justify** your response.

Determine the investment vehicle that would be *most appropriate* for Ælfheah's proposed alternative asset class. (Circle one.)	**Justify** your response.
FOFs	
SMAs	
UCITS	

The following information relates to Questions 19–20

Mbalenhle Calixto is a global institutional portfolio manager who prepares for an annual meeting with the investment committee (IC) of the Estevão University Endowment. The endowment has €450 million in assets, and the current asset allocation is 42% equities, 22% fixed income, 19% private equity, and 17% hedge funds.

The IC's primary investment objective is to maximize returns subject to a given level of volatility. A secondary objective is to avoid a permanent loss of capital, and the IC has indicated to Calixto its concern about left-tail risk. Calixto considers two asset allocation approaches for the endowment: mean–variance optimization (MVO) and mean–CVaR (conditional value at risk) optimization.

19. **Determine** the asset allocation approach that is *most suitable* for the Endowment. **Justify** your response.

Determine the asset allocation approach that is *most suitable* for the Endowment. (Circle one.)	**Justify** your response.
MVO	
Mean–CVaR optimization	

Calixto reviews the endowment's future liquidity requirements and analyzes one of its holdings in a private distressed debt fund. He notes the following about the fund:

- As of the most recent year end:
  - The NAV of the endowment's investment in the fund was €25,000,000.
  - All capital had been called.
- At the end of the current year, Calixto expects a distribution of 18% to be paid.
- Calixto estimates an expected growth rate of 11% for the fund.

20. **Calculate** the expected NAV of the fund at the end of the current year.

CHAPTER 9

EXCHANGE-TRADED FUNDS: MECHANICS AND APPLICATIONS

LEARNING OUTCOMES

The candidate should be able to:

- explain the creation/redemption process of ETFs and the function of authorized participants;
- describe how ETFs are traded in secondary markets;
- describe sources of tracking error for ETFs;
- describe factors affecting ETF bid–ask spreads;
- describe sources of ETF premiums and discounts to NAV;
- describe costs of owning an ETF;
- describe types of ETF risk;
- identify and describe portfolio uses of ETFs.

SUMMARY

In this chapter, we have examined important considerations for ETF investors, including how ETFs work and trade, tax efficient attributes, and key portfolio uses. The following is a summary of key points:

- ETFs rely on a creation/redemption mechanism that allows for the continuous creation and redemption of ETF shares.
- The only investors who can create or redeem new ETF shares are a special group of institutional investors called authorized participants.

- ETFs trade on both the primary market (directly between APs and issuers) and on the secondary markets (exchange-based or over-the-counter trades like listed equity).
- End investors trade ETFs on the secondary markets, like stocks.
- Holding period performance deviations (tracking differences) are more useful than the standard deviation of daily return differences (tracking error).
- ETF tracking differences from the index occur for the following reasons:
  - fees and expenses,
  - representative sampling/optimization,
  - use of depositary receipts and other ETFs,
  - index changes,
  - fund accounting practices,
  - regulatory and tax requirements, and
  - asset manager operations.

- ETFs are generally taxed like the securities they hold, with some nuances:
  - ETFs are more tax fair than traditional mutual funds, because portfolio trading is generally not required when money enters or exits an ETF.
  - Owing to the creation/redemption process, ETFs can be more tax efficient than mutual funds.
  - ETF issuers can redeem out low-cost-basis securities to minimize future taxable gains.
  - Local markets have unique ETF taxation issues that should be considered.

- ETF bid–ask spreads vary by trade size and are usually published for smaller trade sizes. They are tightest for ETFs that are very liquid and have continuous two-way order flow. For less liquid ETFs, the following factors can determine the quoted bid–ask spread of an ETF trade:
  - Creation/redemption costs, brokerage and exchange fees
  - Bid–ask spread of underlying securities held by the ETF
  - Risk of hedging or carry positions by liquidity provider
  - Market makers' target profit spread

- ETF bid–ask spreads on fixed income relative to equity tend to be wider because the underlying bonds trade in dealer markets and hedging is more difficult. Spreads on ETFs holding international stocks are tightest when the underlying security markets are open for trading.
- ETF premiums and discounts refer to the difference between the exchange price of the ETF and the fund's calculated NAV, based on the prices of the underlying securities and weighted by the portfolio positions at the start of each trading day. Premiums and discounts can occur because NAVs are based on the last traded prices, which may be observed at a time lag to the ETF price, or because the ETF is more liquid and more reflective of current information and supply and demand than the underlying securities in rapidly changing markets.
- Costs of ETF ownership may be positive or negative and include both explicit and implicit costs. The main components of ETF cost are
  - the fund management fee;
  - tracking error;
  - portfolio turnover;
  - trading costs, such as commissions, bid–ask spreads, and premiums/discounts;

- taxable gains/losses; and
- security lending.

- Trading costs are incurred when the position is entered and exited. These one-time costs decrease as a portion of total holding costs over longer holding periods and are a more significant consideration for shorter-term tactical ETF traders.
- Other costs, such as management fees and portfolio turnover, increase as a proportion of overall cost as the investor holding period lengthens. These costs are a more significant consideration for longer-term buy-and-hold investors.
- ETFs are different from exchange-traded notes, although both use the creation/redemption process.
  - Exchange-traded notes carry unique counterparty risks of default.
  - Swap-based ETFs may carry counterparty risk.
  - ETFs, like mutual funds, may lend their securities, creating risk of counterparty default.
  - ETF closures can create unexpected tax liabilities.

- ETFs are used for core asset class exposure, multi-asset, dynamic, and tactical strategies based on investment views or changing market conditions; for factor or smart beta strategies with a goal to improve return or modify portfolio risk; and for portfolio efficiency applications, such as rebalancing, liquidity management, completion strategies, and transitions.
- ETFs are useful for investing cash inflows, as well as for raising proceeds to provide for client withdrawals. ETFs are used for rebalancing to target asset class weights and for "completion strategies" to fill a temporary gap in an asset class category, sector, or investment theme or when external managers are underweight. When positions are in transition from one external manager to another, ETFs are often used as the temporary holding and may be used to fund the new manager.
- All types of investors use ETFs to establish low-cost core exposure to asset classes, equity style benchmarks, fixed-income categories, and commodities.
- For more tactical investing, thematic ETFs are used in active portfolio management and represent narrow or niche areas of the equity market not well represented by industry or sector ETFs.
- Systematic, active strategies that use rules-based benchmarks for exposure to such factors as size, value, momentum, quality, or dividend tilts or combinations of these factors are frequently implemented with ETFs.
- Multi-asset and global asset allocation or macro strategies that manage positions dynamically as market conditions change are also areas where ETFs are frequently used.
- Proper utilization requires investors to carefully research and assess the ETF's index construction methodology, costs, risks, and performance history.

PRACTICE PROBLEMS

1. Which of the following statements regarding exchange-traded funds (ETFs) is *correct*? ETFs:
   A. disclose their holdings on a quarterly basis.
   B. trade in both primary and secondary markets.
   C. offer a creation/redemption mechanism that allows any investor to create or redeem shares.

2. The list of securities that a particular ETF wants to own, which is disclosed daily by all ETFs, is referred to as the:
   A. creation unit.
   B. creation basket.
   C. redemption basket.

3. When an authorized participant transacts to create or redeem ETF shares, the related costs are ultimately borne:
   A. solely by the ETF sponsor.
   B. solely by the AP.
   C. proportionally by all existing ETF shareholders.

4. Assuming arbitrage costs are minimal, which of the following is *most likely* to occur when the share price of an ETF is trading at a premium to its intraday NAV?
   A. New ETF shares will be created by the ETF sponsor.
   B. Redemption baskets will be received by APs from the ETF sponsor.
   C. Retail investors will exchange baskets of securities that the ETF tracks for creation units.

5. An ETF's reported tracking error is typically measured as the:
   A. standard deviation of the difference in daily returns between an ETF and its benchmark.
   B. difference in annual return between an ETF and its benchmark over the past 12 months.
   C. annualized standard deviation of the difference in daily returns between an ETF and its benchmark.

6. To best assess an ETF's performance, which reflects the impact of portfolio rebalancing expenses and other fees, an investor should:
   A. review daily return differences between the ETF and its benchmark.
   B. perform a rolling return assessment between the ETF and its benchmark.
   C. compare the ETF's annual expense ratio with that of other ETFs in its asset class category.

7. An ETF's tracking error, as traditionally reported, indicates to investors:
   A. whether the ETF is underperforming or outperforming its underlying index.
   B. the magnitude by which an ETF's returns deviate from its benchmark over time.
   C. the distribution of differences in daily returns between the ETF and its benchmark.

8. For a typical ETF, which of the following sources of tracking error is *most likely* to be the smallest contributor to tracking error?
   A. Representative sampling
   B. Fees and expenses incurred by the ETF
   C. Changes to the underlying index securities

9. Which of the following statements relating to capital gains in ETFs and mutual funds is *correct?*
   A. ETFs tend to distribute less in capital gains than mutual funds do.
   B. Mutual funds may elect not to distribute all realized capital gains in a given year.
   C. The selling of ETF shares by some investors may create capital gains that affect the remaining ETF investors in terms of taxes.

10. Which of the following statements regarding distributions made by ETFs is *correct*?
    A. Return-of-capital (ROC) distributions are generally not taxable.
    B. ETFs generally reinvest any dividends received back into the ETF's holdings.
    C. A dividend distribution is a distribution paid to investors in excess of an ETF's earnings.

11. Such factors as regulations, competition, and corporate actions relate to:
    A. fund-closure risk.
    B. counterparty risk.
    C. expectation-related risk.

12. John Smith has invested in an inverse ETF. Smith is a novice investor who is not familiar with inverse ETFs, and therefore, he is unsure how the ETF will perform because of a lack of understanding of the ETF's risk and return characteristics. This risk is *best* described as:
    A. counterparty risk.
    B. holdings-based risk.
    C. expectation-related risk.

13. Investors buying ETFs:
    A. incur management fees that decrease with the length of the holding period.
    B. are assured of paying a price equal to the NAV if they purchase shares at the market close.
    C. incur trading costs in the form of commissions and bid–ask spreads at the time of purchase.

14. Consider an ETF with the following trading costs and management fees:
    • Annual management fee of 0.40%
    • Round-trip trading commissions of 0.55%
    • Bid–offer spread of 0.20% on purchase and sale
    Excluding compound effects, the expected total holding-period cost for investing in the ETF over a nine-month holding period is *closest* to:
    A. 1.05%.
    B. 1.15%.
    C. 1.25%.

15. The bid–ask spread for very liquid, high-volume ETFs will be *least* influenced by the:
    A. market maker's desired profit spread.
    B. creation/redemption fees and other direct costs.
    C. likelihood of receiving an offsetting ETF order in a short time frame.

16. Factor (smart beta) strategy ETFs are *least likely* to be used by investors:
    A. to modify portfolio risk.
    B. for tactical trading purposes.
    C. to seek outperformance versus a benchmark.

17. Which of the following statements regarding applications of ETFs in portfolio management is correct?
    A. Equity ETFs tend to be more active than fixed-income ETFs.
    B. The range of risk exposures available in the futures market is more diverse than that available in the ETF space.
    C. ETFs that have the highest trading volumes in their asset class category are generally preferred for tactical trading applications.

The following information relates to questions 18–23

Howie Rutledge is a senior portfolio strategist for an endowment fund. Rutledge meets with recently hired junior analyst Larry Stosur to review the fund's holdings.

Rutledge asks Stosur about the mechanics of exchange-traded funds (ETFs). Stosur responds by making the following statements:

Statement 1.   Unlike mutual fund shares that can be shorted, ETF shares cannot be shorted.
Statement 2.   In the ETF creation/redemption process, the authorized participants (APs) absorb the costs of transacting securities for the ETF's portfolio.
Statement 3.   If ETF shares are trading at a discount to NAV and arbitrage costs are sufficiently low, APs will buy the securities in the creation basket and exchange them for ETF shares from the ETF sponsor.

Rutledge notes that one holding, ETF 1, is trading at a premium to its intraday NAV. He reviews the ETF's pricing and notes that the premium to the intraday NAV is greater than the expected arbitrage costs.

Stosur is evaluating three ETFs for potential investment. He notes that the ETFs have different portfolio characteristics that are likely to affect each ETF's tracking error. A summary of the characteristics for the ETFs is presented in Exhibit 1.

EXHIBIT 1   ETF Characteristics Affecting Tracking Error

	ETF 2	ETF 3	ETF 4
Portfolio Construction Approach	Full Replication	Representative Sampling	Full Replication
Type of Foreign Holdings	Local shares	ADRs*	ADRs*
Engagement in Securities Lending	Yes	Yes	No

*ADRs are American Depositary Receipts.

Rutledge and Stosur discuss the factors that influence ETF bid–ask spreads. Stosur tells Rutledge that quoted bid–ask spreads for a particular transaction size are (1) negatively related to the amount of the ongoing order flow in the ETF, (2) positively related to the costs and risks for the ETF liquidity provider, and (3) positively related to the amount of competition among market makers for the ETF.

As ETF shares may trade at prices that are different from the NAV, Rutledge examines selected data in Exhibit 2 for three ETFs that might have this problem.

EXHIBIT 2   Selected Data on ETFs

	ETF 5	ETF 6	ETF 7
Percentage of Foreign Holdings	10%	50%	90%
Trading Frequency	High	Low	Low

Rutledge considers a new ETF investment for the fund. He plans to own the ETF for nine months. The ETF has the following trading costs and management fees:

- Annual management fee of 0.32%
- Round-trip trading commissions of 0.20%
- Bid–offer spread of 0.10% on purchase and sale

Rutledge asks Stosur to compute the expected total holding period cost for investing in the ETF.

18. Which of Stosur's statements regarding ETF mechanics is correct?
    A. Statement 1
    B. Statement 2
    C. Statement 3

19. Given the current pricing of ETF 1, the *most likely* transaction to occur is that:
    A. new ETF shares will be created by the APs.
    B. redemption baskets will be received by APs from the ETF sponsor.
    C. retail investors will exchange baskets of securities that the ETF tracks for creation units.

20. Which ETF in Exhibit 1 is *most likely* to have the lowest tracking error?
    A. ETF 2
    B. ETF 3
    C. ETF 4

21. Stosur's statement about quoted bid–ask spreads is *incorrect* with respect to the:
    A. amount of the ongoing order flow in the ETF.
    B. costs and risks for the ETF liquidity providers.
    C. amount of competition among market makers for the ETF.

22. Which ETF in Exhibit 2 is *most likely* to trade at the largest premium or discount relative to NAV?
    A. ETF 5
    B. ETF 6
    C. ETF 7

23. Excluding the compounding effect, the expected total holding period cost for investing in the ETF over a nine-month holding period is *closest* to:
    A. 0.54%.
    B. 0.62%.
    C. 0.64%.

CHAPTER 10

CASE STUDY IN PORTFOLIO MANAGEMENT: INSTITUTIONAL

LEARNING OUTCOMES

The candidate should be able to:

- discuss tools for managing portfolio liquidity risk;
- discuss capture of the illiquidity premium as an investment objective;
- analyze asset allocation and portfolio construction in relation to liquidity needs and risk and return requirements and recommend actions to address identified needs;
- analyze actions in asset manager selection with respect to the Code of Ethics and Standards of Professional Conduct;
- analyze the costs and benefits of derivatives versus cash market techniques for establishing or modifying asset class or risk exposures;
- demonstrate the use of derivatives overlays in tactical asset allocation and rebalancing.

SUMMARY

The QU endowment case study covers important aspects of institutional portfolio management involving the illiquidity premium capture, liquidity management, asset allocation, and the use of derivatives versus the cash market for tactical asset allocation and portfolio rebalancing. In addition, the case examines potential ethical violations in manager selection that can arise in the course of business.

From an asset allocation perspective, the case highlights potential risk and rewards associated with increasing exposure to illiquidity risk through investments like private equity and private real estate. Although this exposure is expected to generate higher returns and more-efficient portfolios in the long run, significant uncertainties are involved both from a modeling and implementation perspective.

PRACTICE PROBLEMS

The following information relates to Questions 1–2

Joe Bookman is a portfolio manager at State Tech University Foundation and is discussing the $900 million university endowment with the investment committee.

Exhibit 1 presents selected data on the current university endowment.

EXHIBIT 1   Selected Data for State Tech University Endowment

Asset Class	Investment Allocation (% of portfolio)	Liquid	Semi-Liquid	Illiquid	Rebalancing Band Policy	Standard Deviation of Returns (annual)
Cash	1%	100%	0%	0%	0% – 15%	1.5%
Fixed Income	24%	100%	0%	0%	20% – 30%	5.9%
Public Equity	39%	50%	50%	0%	30% – 40%	15.4%
Private Equity	21%	0%	0%	100%	20% – 25%	27.2%
Real Assets	15%	0%	50%	50%	10% – 20%	11.7%

The university investment committee is performing its quarterly assessment and requests that Bookman review the rebalancing band policy.

1. **Identify** which asset class(es) Bookman is *most likely* to note as in need of rebalancing band policy adjustment. **Justify** your selection(s).

Identify which asset class(es) Bookman is *most likely* to note as in need of rebalancing band policy adjustment. [Circle choice(s)]	Justify your selection(s).
Cash	
Fixed Income	
Public Equity	
Private Equity	
Real Assets	

The investment committee also asks Bookman to investigate whether the endowment should increase its allocation to illiquid investments to take advantage of higher potential returns. The endowment's liquidity profile policy stipulates that at least 30% of investments must be classified as liquid to support operating expenses; no more than 40% should be classified as illiquid. Bookman decides to perform a bottom-up liquidity analysis to respond to the committee.

2. **Discuss** the elements of Bookman's analysis and the conclusions he will draw from it.

The following information relates to Question 3

Laura Powers is a senior investment analyst at Brotley University Foundation and works for the university endowment. Powers is preparing a recommendation to allocate more funds into illiquid investments for a higher potential return and is discussing the rationale with junior analyst Jasper Heard. Heard makes the following statements to Powers:

Statement 1.   The endowment should shift funds into private equity and real estate. Specifically, within these asset classes the endowment should target shorter-term investments. These tend to be the most illiquid and offer the highest liquidity premium.

Statement 2.   The endowment should consider low liquidity public equity investments because they are shown to be close substitutes for private equity and real estate investments in terms of liquidity premium.

3.   **Determine if** Heard's statements are correct. **Justify** your response.

Determine if Heard's statements are correct.

Statement 1 (Circle one)	Statement 2 (Circle one)
Correct Incorrect	Correct Incorrect
Justify your response.	**Justify** your response.

The following information relates to Questions 4–5

Rob Smith, as portfolio manager at Pell Tech University Foundation, is responsible for the university's $3.5 billion endowment. The endowment supports the majority of funding for the university's operating budget and financial aid programs. It is invested in fixed income, public equities, private equities, and real assets.

The Pell Tech Board is conducting its quarterly strategic asset allocation review. The board members note that while performance has been satisfactory, they have two concerns:

1. Endowment returns have underperformed in comparison to university endowments of similar size.
2. Return expectations have shifted lower for fixed-income and public equity investments.

Smith attributes this underperformance to a lower risk profile relative to its peers due to a lower allocation to illiquid private equity investments. In response to the board's concerns, Smith proposes an increase in the allocation to the private equity asset class. His proposal uses option price theory for valuation purposes and is supported by Monte Carlo simulations.

Exhibit 1 presents selected data on the current university endowment.

EXHIBIT 1   Selected Data for Pell Tech University Endowment

Portfolio Characteristic	Current Allocation	Proposed Allocation
Expected return (next 10 years)	7.8%	8.3%
Standard deviation of returns (annual)	13.2%	13.9%
Sharpe ratio	0.44	0.45
Probability of 30% erosion in purchasing power over 10 years	25%	20%

4. **Discuss** Smith's method for estimating the increase in return expectations derived from increasing the endowment allocation to private equity.
5. **Discuss** *two* reasons why the increased risk profile is appropriate. **Justify** your response.

The following information relates to Questions 6–7

Frank Grides is a portfolio manager for Kemney University Foundation and manages the liquidity profile of the university endowment. This endowment supports some of the funding for the university's operations. It applies the following spending policy designed to produce a 5% long-term spending rate while shielding annual distributions from fluctuations in its market value:

Spending for current fiscal year = (60% × Spending for previous fiscal year) + [40% × (5% × Endowment market value at the end of previous fiscal year)].

Grides is considering allocating more funds to illiquid investments to capture higher potential returns and is discussing this strategy with senior analyst Don Brodka. Brodka has three related concerns given that the higher allocation to illiquid investments may

- reduce the liquidity profile of the endowment,
- induce "drift" in the portfolio's risk profile in times of market stress, or
- alter the endowment's overall risk profile.

Assessing his concerns, Brodka performs a stress test on the portfolio with both current and proposed investments.
Exhibit 1 presents selected data on the university endowment.

EXHIBIT 1   Selected Data for Kemney University Endowment

Liquidity Category	Current Portfolio: Normal	Current Portfolio: Stress	Proposed Portfolio: Normal	Proposed Portfolio: Stress
Liquid	42%	38%	37%	33%
Semi-liquid	31%	28%	31%	28%
Illiquid	27%	34%	32%	39%

6. **Discuss** the relevance of the endowment's spending policy to Brodka's expressed concerns.
7. **Discuss** actions that Grides should take to alleviate Brodka's concerns.

The following information relates to Question 8

Mason Dixon, CFA, a portfolio manager with Langhorne Advisors (Langhorne), has just completed the request for proposal (RFP) for the Academe Foundation's (the Foundation) $20 million fixed-income mandate. In the performance section of the RFP, Dixon indicated that Langhorne Advisors is a member firm of CFA Institute and has prepared and presented this performance report in compliance with the Global Investment Performance Standards (the GIPS® standards). The performance report presented Langhorne's fixed-income composite returns on the actual net-of fees basis and benchmark returns net of Langhorne's highest scheduled fee (1.00% on the first $5 million; 0.60% thereafter). The report also indicated that as of the most recent quarter, the composite comprised 10 portfolios totaling $600 million of assets under management (AUM).

Upon returning the completed RFP, Dixon thanked the Foundation's chief investment officer, who is also a charterholder, for considering Langhorne. Dixon also indicated that regardless of the outcome of the manager search, he would like to have the CIO and the Foundation's president join him on Langhorne's corporate jet to spend a day at an exclusive California golf club where the firm maintains a corporate membership.

8. **Identify** the ethical concerns posed by Dixon's actions and conduct.

The following information relates to Question 9

In its quarterly policy and performance review, the investment team for the Peralandra University endowment identified a tactical allocation opportunity in international developed equities. The team also decided to implement a passive 1% overweight ($5 million notional value) position in the asset class. Implementation will occur by either using an MISC EAFE Index ETF in the cash market or the equivalent futures contract in the derivatives market.

The team determined that the unlevered cost of implementation is 27 basis points in the cash market (ETF) and 32 bps in the derivatives market (futures). This modest cost differential prompted a comparison of costs on a levered basis to preserve liquidity for upcoming capital commitments in the fund's alternative investment asset classes. For the related analysis, the team's assumptions are as follows:

- Investment policy compliant at 3 times leverage
- Investment horizon of one year
- 3-month Libor of 1.8%
- ETF borrowing cost of 3-month Libor plus 35 bps

9. **Recommend** the most cost-effective strategy. **Justify** your response with calculations of the total levered cost of each implementation option.

The following information relates to Question 10

Clive Staples is a consultant with the Leedsford Organization (Leedsford), a boutique investment consulting firm serving large endowments and private foundations. Leedsford consults on tactical asset allocation (TAA) program development, implementation, and ongoing TAA idea generation.

Staples has just completed his quarterly client review of the Narnea Foundation. Based on the Foundation's current asset allocation and Leedsford's updated fair value models, Staples believes there is an exploitable TAA opportunity in US large-cap growth stocks. He recommends a 2% overweight position to the US equities policy allocation either through an unlevered ETF or total return swap exposures to the Russell 1000 Growth Index.

10. **Compare** the efficiency of the ETF and total return swap TAA implementation alternatives from the perspectives of capital commitment, liquidity, and tracking error.

Compare the efficiency of the ETF and total return swap TAA implementation alternatives from the perspectives of capital commitment, liquidity, and tracking error.

Capital Commitment:

Liquidity:

Tracking Error:

The following information relates to Question 11

The Lemont Family Foundation follows a systematic quarterly rebalancing policy based on rebalancing corridors for each asset class. In the latest quarter, a significant sell-off in US public equities resulted in an unusually large 1.2% underweight position relative to the applicable lower corridor boundary. This is the only policy exception requiring rebalancing attention.

The Foundation's investment team views the sell-off as temporary and remains pleased with the performance of all external managers, including that of its US public equities manager. However, the sell-off has increased the significance of liquidity and flexibility for the team. As a result, the team now considers whether to rebalance through the cash market or the derivatives market.

11. **Determine** the *most appropriate* rebalancing choice for the Foundation's investment team. **Justify** your response.

Determine the *most appropriate* rebalancing choice for the Foundation's investment team. (Circle one)

Cash Market	Derivatives Market

Justify your response.

PART II

SOLUTIONS

CHAPTER 1

BASICS OF PORTFOLIO PLANNING AND CONSTRUCTION

SOLUTIONS

1. C is correct. Depending on circumstances, a written IPS or its equivalent may be required by law or regulation and a written IPS is certainly consistent with best practices. The mere fact that a written IPS is prepared for a client, however, does not *ensure* that risk and return objectives will in fact be achieved.

2. A is correct. A written IPS is best seen as a communication instrument allowing clients and portfolio managers to mutually establish investment objectives and constraints.

3. B is correct. A written IPS, to be successful, must incorporate a full understanding of the client's situation and requirements. As stated in the chapter, "The IPS is typically developed following a fact-finding discussion with the client."

4. B is correct. The major components of an IPS are listed in Section 2.2 of the chapter. *Investment Guidelines* are described as the section that provides information about how policy may be executed, including restrictions on the permissible use of leverage and derivatives and on specific types of assets excluded from investment, if any. *Statement of Duties and Responsibilities* "detail[s] the duties and responsibilities of the client, the custodian of the client's assets, the investment managers, and so forth." *Investment Objectives* is "a section explaining the client's objectives in investing."

5. C is correct. The major components of an IPS are listed in Section 2.2 of the chapter. Strategic Asset Allocation (also known as the policy portfolio) and Rebalancing Policy are often included as appendices to the IPS. The *Statement of Duties and Responsibilities*, however, is an integral part of the IPS and is unlikely to be placed in an appendix.

6. B is correct. According to the chapter, "The sections [of an IPS] that are most closely linked to the client's distinctive needs … are those dealing with investment objectives and constraints." *Investment Guidelines* "[provide] information about how policy

should be executed [including investment constraints]." *Procedures* "[detail] the steps to take to keep the IPS current and the procedures to follow to respond to various contingencies." *Statement of Duties and Responsibilities* "details the duties and responsibilities of the client, the custodian of the client's assets, and the investment managers."

7. A is correct. Because the return objective specifies a target return *relative to* the FTSE 100 Index, the objective is best described as a relative return objective.

8. C is correct. Risk attitude is a subjective factor and measuring risk attitude is difficult. Oftentimes, investment managers use psychometric questionnaires, such as those developed by Grable and Joo (2004), to assess a client's willingness to take risk.

9. B is correct. The reference to the DAX marks this response as a relative risk objective. Value at risk establishes a minimum value of loss expected during a specified time period at a given level of probability. A statement of maximum allowed absolute loss (€2.5 million) is an absolute risk objective.

10. C is correct. Measuring willingness to take risk (risk tolerance, risk aversion) is an exercise in applied psychology. Instruments attempting to measure risk attitudes exist, but they are clearly less objective than measurements of ability to take risk. Ability to take risk is based on relatively objective traits such as expected income, time horizon, and existing wealth relative to liabilities.

11. A is correct. The volatility of the client's income and the significant support needs for his mother and himself suggest that the client has a low ability to take risk. The client's trading experience and his responses to the risk assessment questionnaire indicate that the client has an above average willingness to take risk.

12. B is correct. On the one hand, the client has a stable, high income and no dependents. On the other hand, she exhibits above average risk aversion. Her ability to take risk is high, but her willingness to take risk is low.

13. A is correct. The client's financial objectives are long term. Her stable employment indicates that her immediate liquidity needs are modest. The children will not go to college until 10 or more years later. Her time horizon is best described as being long term.

14. B is correct. The unpredictable nature of property and casualty (P&C) claims forces P&C insurers to allocate a substantial proportion of their investments into liquid, short maturity assets. This need for liquidity also forces P&C companies to accept investments with relatively low expected returns. Liquidity is of less concern to life insurance companies given the greater predictability of life insurance payouts.

15. B is correct. When a client has a restriction in trading, such as this obligation to refrain from trading, the IPS "should note this constraint so that the portfolio manager does not inadvertently trade the stock on the client's behalf."

16. A is correct. The correlation between US equities and Brazilian equities is 0.76. The correlations between US equities and East Asian equities and the correlation between US equities and European equities both exceed 0.76. Lower correlations indicate a greater degree of separation between asset classes. Therefore, using solely the data given in the table, returns on Brazilian equities are most sharply distinguished from returns on US equities.

17. C is correct. Strategic asset allocation depends on several principles. As stated in the chapter, "One principle is that a portfolio's systematic risk accounts for most of its change in value over the long term." A second principle is that, "the returns to groups of similar assets ... predictably reflect exposures to certain sets of systematic factors." This

latter principle establishes that returns on asset classes primarily reflect the systematic risks of the classes.

18. C is correct. As the chapter states, "an asset class should contain relatively homogeneous assets... paired correlations of assets should be relatively high within an asset class but should be lower versus assets in other asset classes."

19. B is correct. Tactical asset allocation allows actual asset allocation to deviate from that of the strategic asset allocation (policy portfolio) of the IPS. Tactical asset allocation attempts to take advantage of temporary dislocations from the market conditions and assumptions that drove the policy portfolio decision.

CHAPTER 2

SECURITY MARKET INDEXES

SOLUTIONS

1. C is correct. A security market index represents the value of a given security market, market segment, or asset class.

2. A is correct. Security market indexes are constructed and managed like a portfolio of securities.

3. A is correct. The first decision is identifying the target market that the index is intended to represent because the target market determines the investment universe and the securities available for inclusion in the index.

4. C is correct. The difference between a price return index and a total return index consisting of identical securities and weights is the income generated over time by the underlying securities. If the securities in the index do not generate income, both indexes will be identical in value.

5. A is correct. At inception, the values of the price return and total return versions of an index are equal.

6. B is correct. The price return is the sum of the weighted returns of each security. The return of Able is 20 percent [(12 − 10)/10]; of Baker is −5 percent [(19 − 20)/20]; and of Charlie is 0 percent [(30 − 30)/30]. The price return index assigns a weight of 1/3 to each asset; therefore, the price return is 1/3 × [20% + (−5%) + 0%] = 5%.

7. C is correct. The total return of an index is calculated on the basis of the change in price of the underlying securities plus the sum of income received or the sum of the weighted total returns of each security. The total return of Able is 27.5 percent; of Baker is 0 percent; and of Charlie is 6.7 percent:
   Able: (12 − 10 + 0.75)/10 = 27.5%
   Baker: (19 − 20 + 1)/20 = 0%
   Charlie: (30 − 30 + 2)/30 = 6.7%
   An equal-weighted index applies the same weight (1/3) to each security's return; therefore, the total return = 1/3 × (27.5% + 0% + 6.7%) = 11.4%.

8. B is correct. The price return of the price-weighted index is the percentage change in price of the index: (68 − 75)/75 = −9.33%.

101

Security	Beginning of Period Price (£)	End of Period Price (£)
ABC	25.00	27.00
DEF	35.00	25.00
GHI	15.00	16.00
TOTAL	75.00	68.00

9. B is correct. The price return of the index is $(48,250,000 - 53,750,000)/53,750,000 = -10.23\%$.

Security	Beginning of Period Price (¥)	Shares Outstanding	Beginning of Period Value (¥)	End of Period Price (¥)	End of Period Value (¥)
MNO	2,500	5,000	12,500,000	2,700	13,500,000
QRS	3,500	7,500	26,250,000	2,500	18,750,000
XYZ	1,500	10,000	15,000,000	1,600	16,000,000
Total			53,750,000		48,250,000

10. B is correct. The total return of the market-capitalization-weighted index is calculated below:

Security	Beginning of Period Value (¥)	End of Period Value (¥)	Total Dividends (¥)	Total Return (%)
MNO	12,500,000	13,500,000	500,000	12.00
QRS	26,250,000	18,750,000	1,125,000	−24.29
XYZ	15,000,000	16,000,000	1,000,000	13.33
Total	53,750,000	48,250,000	2,625,000	−5.35

11. A is correct. The target market determines the investment universe and the securities available for inclusion in the index.

12. A is correct. The sum of prices at the beginning of the period is 96; the sum at the end of the period is 100. Regardless of the divisor, the price return is $100/96 - 1 = 0.042$ or 4.2 percent.

13. B is correct. It is the percentage change in the market value over the period:
Market value at beginning of period: $(20 \times 300) + (50 \times 300) + (26 \times 2,000) = 73,000$
Market value at end of period: $(22 \times 300) + (48 \times 300) + (30 \times 2,000) = 81,000$
Percentage change is $81,000/73,000 - 1 = 0.1096$ or 11.0 percent with rounding.

14. C is correct. With an equal-weighted index, the same amount is invested in each security. Assuming $1,000 is invested in each of the three stocks, the index value is $3,000 at the beginning of the period and the following number of shares is purchased for each stock:
Security A: 50 shares
Security B: 20 shares
Security C: 38.46 shares.

Using the prices at the beginning of the period for each security, the index value at the end of the period is $3,213.8: ($22 × 50) + ($48 × 20) + ($30 × 38.46). The price return is $3,213.8/$3,000 − 1 = 7.1%.

15. A is correct. In the price weighting method, the divisor must be adjusted so the index value immediately after the split is the same as the index value immediately prior to the split.

16. C is correct. The main source of return differences arises from outperformance of small-cap securities or underperformance of large-cap securities. In an equal-weighted index, securities that constitute the largest fraction of the market are underrepresented and securities that constitute only a small fraction of the market are overrepresented. Thus, higher equal-weighted index returns will occur if the smaller-cap equities outperform the larger-cap equities.

17. C is correct. "Float" is the number of shares available for public trading.

18. B is correct. Fundamental weighting leads to indexes that have a value tilt.

19. C is correct. Rebalancing refers to adjusting the weights of constituent securities in an index to maintain consistency with the index's weighting method.

20. B is correct. Changing market prices will cause weights that were initially equal to become unequal, thus requiring rebalancing.

21. C is correct. Reconstitution is the process by which index providers review the constituent securities, re-apply the initial criteria for inclusion in the index, and select which securities to retain, remove, or add. Constituent securities that no longer meet the criteria are replaced with securities that do. Thus, reconstitution reduces the likelihood that the index includes securities that are not representative of the target market.

22. C is correct. Security market indexes play a critical role as proxies for asset classes in asset allocation models.

23. A is correct. Security market indexes are used as proxies for measuring market or systematic risk, not as measures of systemic risk.

24. B is correct. Sector indexes provide a means to determine whether a portfolio manager is more successful at stock selection or sector allocation.

25. C is correct. Style indexes represent groups of securities classified according to market capitalization, value, growth, or a combination of these characteristics.

26. A is correct. The large number of fixed-income securities—combined with the lack of liquidity of some securities—makes it costly and difficult for investors to replicate fixed-income indexes.

27. C is correct. An aggregate fixed-income index can be subdivided by market sector (government, government agency, collateralized, corporate), style (maturity, credit quality), economic sector, or some other characteristic to create more narrowly defined indexes.

28. C is correct. Coupon frequency is not a dimension on which fixed-income indexes are based.

29. A is correct. Commodity indexes consist of futures contracts on one or more commodities.

30. C is correct. The performance of commodity indexes can be quite different from that of the underlying commodities because the indexes consist of futures contracts on the commodities rather than the actual commodities.

31. B is correct. It is not a real estate index category.

32. B is correct. Hedge funds are not required to report their performance to any party other than their investors. Therefore, each hedge fund decides to which database(s) it will report its performance. Thus, for a hedge fund index, constituents determine the index rather than index providers determining the constituents.

33. A is correct. Voluntary performance reporting may lead to survivorship bias, and poorer performing hedge funds will be less likely to report their performance.

34. C is correct. The fixed-income market has more issuers and securities than the equity market.

CHAPTER 3

CAPITAL MARKET EXPECTATIONS, PART I: FRAMEWORK AND MACRO CONSIDERATIONS

SOLUTIONS

1. A is correct. Wakuluk started her career when the global markets were experiencing significant volatility and poor returns. She is careful to base her conclusions on objective evidence and analytical procedures to mitigate potential biases, which suggests she is seeking to mitigate an availability bias. Availability bias is the tendency to be overly influenced by events that have left a strong impression and/or for which it is easy to recall an example.

2. B is correct. Wakuluk's approach to economic forecasting utilizes both a structural model (e.g., an econometric model approach) and a diffusion index (e.g., a leading indicator-based approach). However, the two approaches have weaknesses: An econometric model approach may give a false sense of precision, and a leading indicator-based approach can provide false signals. Two strengths of the checklist approach are its flexibility and limited complexity, although one weakness is that it imposes no consistency of analysis across items or at different points in time.

3. B is correct. Country Z is a developing market. Less-developed markets are likely to be undergoing more rapid structural changes, which may require the analyst to make more significant adjustments relative to past trends.

4. A is correct. Country X is predicted to be in the initial recovery phase of the business cycle, which suggests short-term (money market) rates are low or bottoming. Inflation is procyclical. It accelerates in the later stages of the business cycle when the output gap has closed, and it decelerates when a large output gap puts downward pressure on wages and prices, which often happens during a recession or the early years afterward. As long

105

as short-term interest rates adjust with expected inflation, cash is essentially a zero-duration, inflation-protected asset that earns a floating real rate, which is typically procyclical. Wakuluk assumes short-term interest rates adjust with expected inflation and are procyclical. Thus, short-term rates are most likely to be low and bottoming if Country X is in the initial recovery phase of the business cycle.

5. B is correct. Wakuluk's model predicts that Country Z's business cycle is currently in the late upswing phase. In the late upswing phase, interest rates are typically rising as monetary policy becomes more restrictive. Cyclical assets may underperform, whereas the yield curve is expected to continue to flatten.

6. C is correct. Monetary policy has been persistently loose for Country Y, while fiscal policies have been persistently tight. With this combination of persistently loose and tight policies, the impact could lead to higher or lower nominal rates (typically labeled as mid-nominal rates).

7. C is correct. Country Y is expected to significantly increase transfer payments and introduce a more progressive tax regime. Both of these changes are pro-growth government policies and should have a positive impact on the trend rate of growth for a business cycle that is in slowdown or contraction. Transfer payments help mitigate fluctuations in disposable income for the most vulnerable households, while progressive tax regimes imply that the effective tax rate on the private sector is pro-cyclical (i.e., rising as the economy expands and falling as the economy contracts).

8. C is correct. The current yield curve for Country Y suggests that the business cycle is in the slowdown phase (curve is flat to inverted), with bond yields starting to reflect contractionary conditions (i.e., bond yields are declining). The curve will most likely steepen near term, consistent with the transition to the contractionary phase of the business cycle, and be the steepest on the cusp of the initial recovery phase.

9. The process of setting capital market expectations (CMEs) involves the following seven steps:

    A. Specify the set of expectations needed, including the time horizon(s) to which they apply.
    B. Research the historical record.
    C. Specify the method(s) and/or model(s) to be used and their information requirements.
    D. Determine the best sources for information needs.
    E. Interpret the current investment environment using the selected data and methods, applying experience and judgment.
    F. Provide the set of expectations needed, documenting conclusions.
    G. Monitor actual outcomes and compare them with expectations, providing feedback to improve the expectation-setting process.

    The first step, which specifies the set of expectations needed, is carried out by the firm. Wuyan, in developing a statistical model based on a dividend discount method, researched the historical data seeking to identify the relevant variables and determined the best source of data for the model. In her report, she also noted her interpretation of the current economic and market environment. To complete the process, Wuyan should complete Steps 6 and 7. Wuyan should provide the set of expectations needed, documenting the conclusions, and include the reasoning and assumptions underlying the projections. Then, she should monitor the actual outcomes and compare them with the expectations, providing feedback to assess and improve the accuracy of the process.

The comparison of the capital market expectations estimated by the model against actual results provides a quantitative evaluation of forecast error. The feedback from this step can be used to improve the expectation-setting process.

10. **Discuss** how *each* of the following forecasting challenges evident in Wuyan's report and in Tommanson's comments affects the setting of capital market expectations:

Status quo bias	Tommanson's statement that he is reluctant to underweight equities given the strong performance of equities over the last quarter is an example of status quo bias. His statement that the most recent quarterly data should be weighted more heavily in setting capital market expectations is also an example of this bias. Status quo bias reflects the tendency for forecasts to perpetuate recent observations and for managers to then avoid making changes. Status quo bias can be mitigated by a disciplined effort to avoid anchoring on the status quo.
Data-mining bias	In Wuyan's report, data-mining bias arises from repeatedly searching a data set until a statistically significant pattern emerges. Such a pattern will almost inevitably occur, but the statistical relationship cannot be expected to have predictive value. As a result, the modeling results are unreliable. Irrelevant variables are often included in the forecasting model. As a solution, the analyst should scrutinize the variables selected and provide an economic rationale for each variable selected in the forecasting model. A further test is to examine the forecasting relationship out of sample.
Risk of regime change	The suggestion by Tommanson to extend the data series back increases the risk of the data representing more than one regime. A change in regime is a shift in the technological, political, legal, economic, or regulatory environments. Regime change alters the risk–return relationship since the asset's risk and return characteristics vary with economic and market environments. Analysts can apply statistical techniques that account for the regime change or simply use only part of the whole data series.
Misinterpretation of correlation	Wuyan states that the high correlation between nominal GDP and equity returns implies nominal GDP predicts equity returns. This statement is incorrect since high correlation does not imply causation. In this case, nominal GDP could predict equity returns, equity returns could predict nominal GDP, a third variable could predict both, or the relationship could merely be spurious. Correlation does not allow the analyst to distinguish between these cases. As a result, correlation relationships should not be used in a predictive model without understanding the underlying linkages between the variables.

11. The growth rate in the aggregate market value of equity is expressed as a sum of the following four factors: (1) growth rate of nominal GDP, (2) the change in the share of profits in GDP, (3) the change in P/E, and (4) the dividend yield. The growth rate of nominal GDP is the sum of the growth of real GDP and inflation. The growth rate of real GDP is estimated as the sum of the growth rate in the labor input and the growth rate in labor productivity. Based on the chief economist's estimates, the macroeconomic forecast indicates that nominal GDP will increase by 4.0% (= 0.5% labor input + 1.3% productivity + 2.2% inflation).

Assuming a 2.8% dividend yield and no change in the share of profits in the economy, Cambo's forecast of a 9.0% annual increase in equity returns implies a 2.2% long-term contribution (i.e., 9.0% equity return − 4.0% nominal GDP − 2.8% dividend yield) from an expansion in the P/E.

12. **Discuss**, based on the chief economist's prediction, the implications for the following:

Bond yields	In the late expansion phase of the business cycle, bond yields are usually rising but more slowly than short-term interest rates are, so the yield curve flattens. Private sector borrowing puts upward pressure on rates while fiscal balances typically improve.
Equity returns	In the late expansion phase of the business cycle, stocks typically rise but are subject to high volatility as investors become nervous about the restrictive monetary policy and signs of a looming economic slowdown. Cyclical assets may underperform while inflation hedges, such as commodities, outperform.
Short-term interest rates	In the late expansion phase of the business cycle, short-term interest rates are typically rising as monetary policy becomes restrictive because the economy is increasingly in danger of overheating. The central bank may aim for a soft landing.

13. **Discuss** strengths and weaknesses of the economic forecasting approaches used by Cambo and the chief economist.

	Cambo's Forecasting Approach	Chief Economist's Forecasting Approach
Strengths	• The leading indicator–based approach is simple since it requires following a limited number of economic/financial variables. • Can focus on individual or composite variables that are readily available and easy to track. • Focuses on identifying/forecasting turning points in the business cycle.	• Econometric models can be quite robust and can examine impact of many potential variables. • New data may be collected and consistently used within models to quickly generate output. • Models are useful for simulating effects of changes in exogenous variables. • Imposes discipline and consistency on the forecaster and challenges modeler to reassess prior view based on model results.
Weaknesses	• Data subject to frequent revisions resulting in "look-ahead" bias. • "Current" data not reliable as input for historical analysis. • Overfitted in sample. Likely overstates forecast accuracy. • Can provide false signals on the economic outlook. • May provide little more than binary directional guidance (no/yes).	• Models are complex and time consuming to formulate. • Requires future forecasts for the exogenous variables, which increases the estimation error for the model. • Model may be mis-specified, and relationships among variables may change over time. • Models may give false sense of precision. • Models perform badly at forecasting turning points.

14. **Discuss** the implications of Hadpret's inflation forecast on the expected returns of the fund's holdings of:

Cash	The fund benefits from its cyclically low holdings of cash. With the economy contracting and inflation falling, short-term rates will likely be in a sharp decline. Cash, or short-term interest-bearing instruments, is unattractive in such an environment. However, deflation may make cash particularly attractive if a "zero lower bound" is binding on the nominal interest rate. Otherwise, deflation is simply a component of the required short-term real rate.
Bonds	The fund's holdings of high-quality bonds will benefit from falling inflation or deflation. Falling inflation results in capital gains as the expected inflation component of bond yields falls. Persistent deflation benefits the highest-quality bonds because it increases the purchasing power of their cash flows. It will, however, impair the creditworthiness of lower-quality debt.
Equities	The fund's holdings of asset-intensive and commodity-producing firms will be negatively affected by falling inflation or deflation. Within the equity market, higher inflation benefits firms with the ability to pass along rising costs. In contrast, falling inflation or deflation is especially detrimental for asset-intensive and commodity-producing firms unable to pass along the price increases.
Real Estate	The fund's real estate holdings will be negatively affected by falling inflation or deflation. Falling inflation or deflation will put downward pressure on expected rental income and property values. Especially negatively affected will be sub-prime properties that may have to cut rents sharply to avoid rising vacancies.

15. Hadpret expects that, in response to a forecasted contraction in the Eastland economy, the central bank will ease monetary policy and the government will enact an expansionary fiscal policy. This policy mix has an impact on the shape of the yield curve.

The impact of changes in monetary policy on the yield curve are fairly clear, because changes in the yield curve's slope—its flattening or steepening—are largely determined by the expected movement in short rates. This movement, in turn, is determined by the expected path of monetary policy and the state of the economy. With the central bank easing and the economy contracting, policy rates will be declining and will be expected to decline further as the central bank aims to counteract downward momentum in the economy. Bond yields also decline but by a lesser amount, so the yield curve steepens. The yield curve will typically continue to steepen during the contraction phase as the central bank continues to ease, reaching its steepest point just before the initial recovery phase.

Fiscal policy may affect the shape of the yield curve through the relative supply of bonds at various maturities that the government issues to fund deficits. Unlike the impact of monetary policy, the impact of changes in the supply of securities on the yield curve is unclear. The evidence seems to suggest that sufficiently large purchases/sales at different maturities will have only a temporary impact on yields. As a result, the large government budget deficits forecasted by Hadpret are unlikely to have much of a lasting impact on the yield curve, especially given that private sector borrowing will be falling during the contraction, somewhat offsetting the increase in the supply of government securities.

16. **Discuss** how interest rate and exchange rate linkages between Eastland and Northland might change under *each* scenario. (Note: Consider *each* scenario independently.)

Scenario 1   Eastland currently has a fixed exchange rate with unrestricted capital flows. It is unable to pursue an independent monetary policy, and interest rates will be equal to those in Northland. By restricting capital flows along with a fixed exchange rate, Eastland will be able to run an independent monetary policy with the central bank setting the policy rate. Thus, interest rates can be different in the two countries.

Scenario 2   Eastland currently has a fixed exchange rate pegged to Northland with unrestricted capital flows. Eastland is unable to pursue an independent monetary policy with interest rates in Eastland equal to the interest rates prevailing in Northland (the country to which the currency is pegged). If Eastland allows the exchange rate to float, it will now be able to run an independent monetary policy with interest rates determined in its domestic market. The link between interest rates and exchange rates will now be largely expectational and will depend on the expected future path of the exchange rate. To equalize risk-adjusted returns across countries, interest rates must generally be higher (lower) in the country whose currency is expected to depreciate (appreciate). This dynamic often leads to a situation where the currency overshoots in one direction or the other.

Scenario 3   Eastland and Northland (with currencies pegged to each other) will share the same yield curve if two conditions are met. First, unrestricted capital mobility must occur between them to ensure that risk-adjusted expected returns will be equalized. Second, the exchange rate between the currencies must be credibly fixed forever. Thus, as long as investors believe that there is no risk in the future of a possible currency appreciation or depreciation, Eastland and Northland will share the same yield curve. A shift in investors' belief in the credibility of the fixed exchange rate will likely cause risk and yield differentials to emerge. This situation will cause the (default-free) yield curve to differ between Eastland and Northland.

CHAPTER 4

CAPITAL MARKET EXPECTATIONS, PART II: FORECASTING ASSET CLASS RETURNS

SOLUTIONS

1. A.

	Risk-free interest rate (nominal) (%)	+ Premiums (%)	=	Expected annual fixed-income return (%)
1-year government bond	3.8	+ 0	=	3.8
10-year government bond	3.8	+ 1	=	4.8
10-year corporate bond	3.8	+ 1 + 0.75 + 0.55	=	6.1

Estimate of the expected return of an equal-weighted investment in the three securities: (3.8% + 4.8% + 6.1%)/3 = 4.9%.

B. The average spread (over 1-year government bond) at issue is [0 + 1 + (1 + 0.75 + 0.55)] = 3.3%/3 = 1.1%.

As the 1.1% is less than 1.5%, the investor will not make the investment.

2. The statement correctly identifies economic, political, and legal risk. The adviser has correctly identified some of the characteristics typically associated with emerging and frontier markets that may affect their governments' and corporate borrowers' ability and willingness to pay bondholders. However, the assertion that all emerging and frontier market fixed-income securities pose such risk is incorrect, as many countries classified as "emerging" are considered to be healthy and prosperous economies.

3. A. The historical equity risk premium is 1.8%, calculated as follows:

Historical equity returns − Historical 10-year government bond yield
    = Historical equity risk premium

4.6% − 2.8% = 1.8%

   B. The Grinold–Kroner model states that the expected return on equity is the sum of the expected income return (2.4%), the expected nominal earnings growth return (7.3% = 2.3% from inflation + 5.0% from real earnings growth), and the expected repricing return (−3.45%). The expected change in market valuation of −3.45% is calculated as the percentage change in the P/E level from the current 14.5× to the expected level of 14.0×: (14 − 14.5)/14.5 = −3.45%. Thus, the expected return is 2.4% + 7.3% − 3.45% = 6.25%.

   C. Using the results from Part B, the expected equity return is 6.25 percent.

Expected equity return − Current 10-year government bond yield
    = Expected equity risk premium

6.25% − 2.3% = 3.95%.

4. A. Using the formula $RP_i^G = \rho_{i,\text{GM}}\sigma_i\left(\frac{RP_{GM}}{\sigma_{GM}}\right)$ we can solve for each expected industry risk premium. The term in parentheses is the Sharpe ratio for the GIM, computed as 3.5/8.5 = 0.412.

   i. $RP_{\text{Health Care}}$ = (12)(0.7)(0.412) = 3.46%
   ii. RP_{Watch} = (6)(0.8)(0.412) = 1.98%
   iii. $RP_{\text{Consumer Products}}$ = (7.5)(0.8)(0.412) = 2.47%

   B. Based on the above analysis, the Swiss Health Care Industry would have the highest expected return. However, that expected return reflects compensation for systematic risk. Based on the data provided we cannot conclude which industry is most attractive from a valuation standpoint.

5. In addition to the economic, political and legal risks faced by fixed-income investors, equity investors in emerging markets face corporate governance risks. Their ownership claims may be expropriated by corporate insiders, dominant shareholders, or the government. Interested parties may misuse the companies' assets. Weak disclosure and accounting standards may result in limited transparency that favors insiders. Weak checks and balances on governmental actions may bring about regulatory uncertainty, seizure of property, or nationalization.

6. Properties trade infrequently so there is no data on simultaneous periodic transaction prices for a selection of properties. Analysis therefore relies on appraisals. Secondly, each property is different; it is said to be heterogenous. The returns calculated from appraisals represent weighted averages of unobservable returns. Published return series is too smooth and the sample volatility understates the true volatility of returns. It also distorts estimates of correlations.

7. The expected change in the cap rate from 5.7% to 5.5% represents a (5.5% − 5.7%)/5.7% = 3.5% decrease.

Using the expression $E(R_{re}) = \text{CapRate} + \text{NOI growth rate} - \%\Delta\text{CapRate} = 5.7\% +$ (1% + 1.5%) − (−3.5%) = 11.7%.

Note: As the cap rate is expected to decrease, property values are expected to increase, hence the cap rate change contributes to the expected return.

8. Under the first approach analysts focus on flows of export and imports to establish what the net trade flows are and how large they are relative to the economy and other, potentially larger financing and investment flows. The approach also considers differences between domestic and foreign inflation rates that relate to the concept of purchasing power parity. Under PPP, the expected percentage change in the exchange rate should equal the difference between inflation rates. The approach also considers the sustainability of current account imbalances, reflecting the difference between national saving and investment.

Under the second approach the analysis focuses on capital flows and the degree of capital mobility. It assumes that capital seeks the highest risk-adjusted return. The expected changes in the exchange rate will reflect the differences in the respective countries' assets' characteristics such as relative short-term interest rates, term, credit, equity, and liquidity premiums. The approach also considers hot money flows and the fact that exchange rates provide an across-the-board mechanism for adjusting the relative sizes of each country's portfolio of assets.

9.

	Country X	Country Y
Expected inflation over next year	2.0%	3.0%
Short-term (1-month) government rate	Decrease	Increase
Expected (forward-looking) GDP growth over next year	2.0%	3.3%
New national laws have been passed that enable foreign direct investment in real estate/financial companies	Yes	No
Current account surplus (deficit)	8%	−1%

Note: The shaded cells represent the comparatively stronger measure, where an analyst could expect to see a strengthening currency based on the factor being independently reviewed.

10. According to PPP, to offset the effect of the higher inflation in Fap, the Fip should have depreciated against the other currencies by approximately the difference between Fap inflation and that in the other countries.

According to PPP, Fip is overvalued.

11. B is correct. Statement 2 is correct because traded REIT securities are more highly correlated with direct real estate and less highly correlated with equities over multi-year horizons. Thus, although REITs tend to act like stocks in the short run, they act like real estate in the longer run.

A and C are incorrect because Statement 1 is not correct. Traded REIT securities have relatively high correlations with equity securities over short time horizons, such as one year. The higher correlations suggest that traded REIT securities will not act as a good diversifier for an equity portfolio over a one-year period.

12. A is correct. An estimate of the long-run expected or required return for commercial real estate equals the sum of the capitalization rate (cap rate) plus the growth rate (constant) of net operating income (NOI). An approximation of the steady-state NOI growth rate for commercial real estate is equal to the growth rate in GDP. Thus, from Equation 7

and the information provided in Exhibit 1, $E(R_{re})$ = Cap rate + NOI growth rate = 4.70% + 4.60% = 9.30%, which is approximately double the cap rate.

B is incorrect because the discount rate (expected or required return) equals the sum of the cap rate and the NOI growth rate. Based on the information in Exhibit 1, the 4.70% cap rate is less than (not greater than) the 9.30% discount rate.

C is incorrect because the discount rate over finite horizons (not long-run horizons) needs to include the anticipated rate of change in the cap rate. For long-run expected return calculations, the anticipated rate of change in the cap rate is not included.

13. C is correct. The in-house model assumes that the current observed return equals the weighted average of the current true return and the previous observed return. The model uses REIT index returns as proxies for the returns in the model. The smoothed nature of most published (observed) real estate returns is a major contributor to the appearance of low correlation with financial assets. This smoothing dampens the volatility of the observed data and distorts correlations with other assets. Thus, the raw observable data tend to understate the risk and overstate the diversification benefits of these asset classes. It is generally accepted that the true variance of real estate returns is greater than the variance of the observed data.

14. B is correct. If the investment horizon equals the (Macaulay) duration of the portfolio, the capital loss created by the increase in yields and the reinvestment effects (gains) will roughly offset, leaving the realized return approximately equal to the original yield to maturity. This relationship is exact if (a) the yield curve is flat and (b) the change in rates occurs immediately in a single step. In practice, the relationship is only an approximation. In the case of the domestic sovereign yield curve, the 20 bp increase in rates will likely be offset by the higher reinvestment rate, creating an annual return approximately equal to 2.00%.

15. A is correct. From the building block approach to fixed-income returns, the required return for fixed-income asset classes has four components: the one-period default-free rate, the term premium, the credit premium, and the liquidity premium. Since sovereign bonds are considered the highest-quality bonds, they likely do not have a significant credit premium nor are they likely to have a significant premium for illiquidity. The slope of the yield curve is useful information on which to base forecasts of the term premium. Therefore, the dominant source of the yield spread is most likely the term premium for XYZ's sovereign bond.

16. A is correct. The credit premium is the additional expected return demanded for bearing the risk of default losses. A credit downgrade two steps lower will increase the credit premium and the required rate of return. The change in the default-free rate associated with the monetary tightening will increase (not decrease) the required rate of return. The widening of the spread between the sovereign bond and the next highest-quality government agency security indicates an increase in the liquidity premium, which will increase (not decrease) the required rate of return.

B is incorrect because the required rate of return would increase (not decrease) based on the change in the default-free rate associated with the monetary tightening.

C is incorrect because the rate of return would increase (not decrease) based on a change in the liquidity premium. The liquidity premium can be estimated from the yield spread between the highest-quality issuer (typically a sovereign bond) and the next highest-quality large issuer of similar bonds (often a government agency). A widening yield spread indicates an increase in the liquidity premium and required rate of return.

17. C is correct. Emerging market debt requires an analysis of economic and political/legal risks. Based on the macroeconomic factors, the risk of a bond investment in either Republic A or Republic B appears to be high. Thresholds such as the risk guidelines listed in the table below can be used to assess the attractiveness of the two emerging market (EM) opportunities in Republic A and Republic B. Most notably, both republics raise concern based solely on their fiscal deficit-to-GDP ratios greater than 4.00% (Republic A's is 6.50% and Republic B's is 8.20%).

Emerging Market Analysis

Country Political/Economic Risk	Emerging Market Risk Guidelines	Emerging Republic A	Emerging Republic B
Fiscal deficit/GDP	4.00%	Negative	Negative
Debt/GDP	70.00%	Negative	Negative
Current account deficit	4.00% of GDP	Negative	Negative
Foreign exchange reserves	100.00% of short-term debt	Negative	Negative

Analysis of the economic and political risks associated with the two EM opportunities is suggestive of the need for further scrutiny; therefore, the foundation should not invest in Emerging Republic A or Emerging Republic B based only on the information provided.

18. C is correct. An investment in the bonds of the international energy exploration and production company (Xdelp) looks attractive. The international market benefits from positive macroeconomic fundamentals: point in the business cycle, monetary and fiscal discipline, rising current account surplus, and an appreciating currency. The anticipated credit rating improvement will add to the potential for this to become a profitable investment and enhance returns. An increase in the investments within the international fixed-income segment by 1.00% (existing weight is 6.17%) would take advantage of this opportunity and remain in compliance with the foundation's 5.00%–10.00% strategic asset allocation limits.

A is incorrect because a decrease in the existing weight of real estate by 2.00% would put the portfolio weight below the minimum threshold of 2.00% (i.e., 3.34% − 2.00% = 1.34%) of the foundation's strategic asset allocation.

B is incorrect because the information presented in Exhibit 3 would lead the chief investment officer to avoid the two opportunities in emerging market debt (Emerging Republic A and Emerging Republic B) and not initiate a commitment to emerging market debt of 1.00% (i.e., increase the existing weight above 0.00%).

19. C is correct. Statement 3 is correct. As long as none of the factors used in a factor-based VCV model are redundant and none of the asset returns are completely determined by the common factors, there will not be any portfolios that erroneously appear to be riskless. Therefore, a factor-based VCV matrix approach may result in some portfolios that erroneously appear to be riskless if any asset returns can be completely determined by the common factors or some of the factors are redundant.

A is incorrect because shrinkage estimation of VCV matrices will increase the efficiency of the estimates versus the sample VCV matrix, because its mean squared error (MSE) will in general be smaller than the MSE of the (unbiased) sample VCV matrix. Efficiency in this context means a smaller MSE.

B is incorrect because, although the proposed approach is not reliable, the reason is not that the sample VCV matrix is biased and inconsistent; on the contrary, it is unbiased and consistent. Rather, the estimate of the VCV matrix is not reliable because the number of observations is not at least 10 times the number of assets (i.e., with 10 years of monthly return data, there are only 120 observations, but the rule of thumb suggests there should be at least 200 observations for 20 asset classes).

20. B is correct. Bader expects the equity market in Country C (an emerging market) to become more fully integrated with the global market while Country A (a developed market) remains highly integrated. All else being equal, the Singer–Terhaar model implies that when a market becomes more globally integrated (segmented), its required return should decline (rise). As prices adjust to a lower (higher) required return, the market should deliver an even higher (lower) return than was previously expected or required by the market. Therefore, the allocation to markets that are moving toward integration should be increased. If a market is moving toward integration, its increased allocation will come at the expense of markets that are already highly integrated. This will typically entail a shift from developed markets to emerging markets.

21. B is correct. Country A's long-term corporate earnings growth rate of 4% per year is equal to the expected nominal GDP growth rate of 4%, which is an economically plausible long-run assumption. The only very long-run assumptions that are consistent with economically plausible relationships are $\%\Delta E$ = Nominal GDP growth, $\%\Delta S$ = 0, and $\%\Delta P/E$ = 0, where $\%\Delta E$ is the expected nominal earnings growth rate, $\%\Delta S$ is the expected percentage change in shares outstanding, and $\%\Delta P/E$ is the expected percentage change in the price-to-earnings ratio.

   A is incorrect because a 2% rate of net share repurchases would eventually eliminate all shares, which is not an economically plausible very long-run assumption. The only very long-run assumptions that are consistent with economically plausible relationships are $\%\Delta E$ = Nominal GDP growth, $\%\Delta S$ = 0, and $\%\Delta P/E$ = 0, where $\%\Delta E$ is the expected nominal earnings growth rate, $\%\Delta S$ is the expected percentage change in shares outstanding, and $\%\Delta P/E$ is the expected percentage change in the price-to-earnings ratio.

   C is incorrect because Country A's perpetually rising P/E would lead to an arbitrarily high price per currency unit of earnings per share. The only very long-run assumptions that are consistent with economically plausible relationships are $\%\Delta E$ = Nominal GDP growth, $\%\Delta S$ = 0, $\%\Delta P/E$ = 0, where $\%\Delta E$ is the expected nominal earnings growth rate, $\%\Delta S$ is the expected percentage change in shares outstanding, and $\%\Delta P/E$ is the expected percentage change in the price-to-earnings ratio.

22. A is correct. Per capita income for Country B has been falling, which is a potential source of political stress.

   B is incorrect because the persistent current account deficit has been below 2% of GDP. Persistent current account deficits greater than 4% of GDP probably indicate a lack of competitiveness.

   C is incorrect because Country B has been transitioning to International Financial Reporting Standards, with full convergence expected within two years, which is a positive development for better accounting standards.

23. A is correct. Bader should reallocate capital from Country A, which is expected to have a secularly rising current account deficit, to Country C, which is expected to have a secularly rising current account surplus. A rising current account deficit will tend to put

upward pressure on real required returns and downward pressure on asset prices, whereas a rising current account surplus (or narrowing deficit) will put downward pressure on real required returns and upward pressure on asset prices. Analysts should consider reallocation of portfolio assets from countries with secularly rising current account deficits to those with secularly rising current account surpluses (or narrowing deficits).

24.   A is correct. Purchasing power parity implies that the value of Country A's currency will decline. Inflation for Country A is expected to rise relative to global inflation. Purchasing power parity implies that the expected percentage change in Country A's exchange rate should be equal to the difference in expected inflation rates. If Country A's inflation is rising relative to global inflation, then the currency will be expected to depreciate.

B is incorrect because purchasing power parity implies that the value of Country B's currency will remain stable. Inflation for Country B is expected to keep pace with global inflation. Purchasing power parity implies that the expected percentage change in Country B's exchange rate should be equal to the difference in expected inflation rates. If Country B's inflation is keeping pace with global inflation, then the exchange rate will be expected to stay the same, corresponding to a stable value of Country B's currency.

C is incorrect because purchasing power parity implies that the value of Country C's currency will rise. Inflation for Country C is expected to fall relative to global inflation. Purchasing power parity implies that the expected percentage change in Country C's exchange rate should be equal to the difference in expected inflation rates. If Country C's inflation is falling relative to global inflation, then the currency will be expected to appreciate.

25.   B is correct. Hot money is flowing out of Country B; thus, Country B's central bank is the most likely to sell foreign currency (thereby draining domestic liquidity) to limit/ avoid depreciation of the domestic currency and buy government securities (thereby providing liquidity) to sterilize the impact on bank reserves and interest rates.

A is incorrect because Country A is not experiencing hot money flows and, therefore, would not need to sterilize the impact of money flows on domestic liquidity.

C is incorrect because hot money is flowing into Country C; thus, Country C's central bank is most likely to sell government securities to limit the growth of bank reserves and/or maintain a target level of interest rates.

26.   C is correct. Public debt makes up the majority of Country C's currency portfolio, which is the least supportive flow (or holding) to a currency. Public debt is less supportive because it has to be serviced and must be either repaid or refinanced, potentially triggering a crisis. Some types of flows and holdings are considered to be more or less supportive of the currency. Investments in private equity represent long-term capital committed to the market and are most supportive of the currency. Public equity would likely be considered the next most supportive of the currency. Debt investments are the least supportive of the currency.

CHAPTER 5

OVERVIEW OF ASSET ALLOCATION

SOLUTIONS

1. A is correct. The Laws' economic net worth is closest to $925,000. An economic balance sheet includes conventional financial assets and liabilities, as well as extended portfolio assets and liabilities that are relevant in making asset allocation decisions. The economic balance sheet for the Law family is shown in the following exhibit.

Assets		Liabilities and Economic Net Worth	
Financial Assets		*Financial Liabilities*	
Fixed income	450,000	Mortgage debt	225,000
Real estate	400,000		
Equity	800,000		
Extended Assets		*Extended Liabilities*	
Human capital	1,025,000	Children's education	275,000
		Endowment funding	500,000
		Present value of consumption	750,000
Total Economic Assets	2,675,000	*Total Economic Liabilities*	1,750,000
		Economic Net Worth	925,000

Economic net worth is equal to total economic assets minus total economic liabilities ($2,675,000 − $1,750,000 = $925,000).

2. A is correct. The Laws' equity portfolio is heavily concentrated in WS stock (80% of the equity portfolio), and both Laws work at WS. Should WS encounter difficult economic circumstances, the investment value of WS stock and the Laws' human capital are both likely to be adversely affected. Thus, their investment in WS should be reviewed and their equity portfolio diversified further.

3. C is correct. In order to effectively specify asset classes for the purpose of asset allocation, assets within an asset class should be relatively homogeneous and have similar attributes. The previous adviser's specification of the debt asset class includes global investment-grade corporate bonds and real estate. This definition results in a non-homogeneous asset class.

4. A is correct. For risk control purposes, an asset class should be diversifying and should not have extremely high expected correlations with other classes. Because the returns to the equity and the derivatives asset classes are noted as being highly correlated, inclusion of both asset classes will result in duplication of risk exposures. Including both asset classes is not diversifying to the asset allocation.

5. B is correct. Raye believes the Laws' previous financial adviser followed an asset allocation approach that resulted in an overlap in risk factors among asset classes. A multifactor risk model approach can be used to address potential risk factor overlaps. Risk factor approaches to asset allocation focus on assigning investments to the investor's desired exposures to specified risk factors. These methods are premised on the observation that asset classes often exhibit some overlaps in sources of risk.

6. A is correct. Portfolio 1 best meets the Laws' education goal for their children. The estimated present value of the Laws' expected education expense is $275,000. Given that the children will be starting college soon, and the Laws have a very strong desire to achieve this goal, Portfolio 1, which stresses liquidity and stability, is most appropriate to meet the Laws' short-term education goal.

7. B is correct. Portfolio 2 best meets the Laws' goal to fund an endowment for their alma mater in 20 years. In present value terms, the gift is valued at $500,000, with the Laws desiring a high probability of achieving this goal. Although slightly more conservative than the 75/25 global equity/bond mix, Portfolio 2 has a greater growth emphasis compared with Portfolios 1 and 3. Therefore, Portfolio 2 is best for funding the endowment at their alma mater given the goal's long-term horizon and the Laws' desire for a high probability of achieving it.

8. B is correct. Using the cost–benefit approach, higher transaction costs for an asset class imply wider rebalancing ranges. Raye's recommendation for a wider rebalancing range for global equities is consistent with the presence of higher transaction costs for global equities.

CHAPTER 6

PRINCIPLES OF ASSET ALLOCATION

SOLUTIONS

1. A is correct. The allocations in Exhibit 1 are most likely from an MVO model using historical data inputs. MVO tends to result in asset allocations that are concentrated in a subset of the available asset classes. The allocations in Exhibit 1 have heavy concentrations in four of the asset classes and no investment in the other four asset classes, and the weights differ greatly from global market weights. Compared to the use of historical inputs, the Black–Litterman and reverse-optimization models most likely would be less concentrated in a few asset classes and less distant from the global weights.

2. A is correct. Theoretically, higher-risk assets would warrant a narrow corridor because high-risk assets are more likely to stray from the desired strategic asset allocation. However, narrow corridors will likely result in more frequent rebalancing and increased transaction costs, so in practice corridor width is often specified to be proportionally greater the higher the asset class's volatility. Thus, higher-risk assets should have a wider corridor to avoid frequent, costly rebalancing costs. Her other suggestions are not correct. Less-liquid asset classes should have a wider, not narrower, corridor width. Less-liquid assets should have a wider corridor to avoid frequent rebalancing costs. For taxable investors, transactions trigger capital gains in jurisdictions that tax them. For such investors, higher tax rates on capital gains should be associated with wider (not narrower) corridor widths.

3. A is correct. The original funding ratio is the market value of assets divided by the present value of liabilities. This plan's ratio is $205 million/$241 million = 0.8506. When the assets and liabilities both decrease by $25 million, the funding ratio will decrease to $180 million/$216 million = 0.8333.

4. B is correct. The objective function expected value is $U_m^{LR} = E(R_{s,m}) - 0.005\lambda\sigma^2(R_{s,m})$. λ is equal to 1.5, and the expected value of the objective function is shown in the rightmost column below.

Portfolio	$E(R_s,m)$	$\sigma^2(R_s,m)$	$U_m^{LR} = E(R_s,m) - 0.005(1.5)\sigma^2(R_s,m)$
1	13.00	576	8.68
2	12.00	324	9.57
3	11.00	361	8.29

Portfolio 2 generates the highest value, or utility, in the objective function.

5. C is correct. The hedging/return-seeking portfolios approach is best for this client. Beade should construct two portfolios, one that includes riskless bonds that will pay off the fixed obligation in 10 years and the other a risky portfolio that earns a competitive risk-adjusted return. This approach is a simple two-step process of hedging the fixed obligation and then investing the balance of the assets in a return-seeking portfolio.

6. A is correct. Goal 1 requires a success rate of at least 95%, and Sub-Portfolio A has the highest minimum expected return (2.05%) meeting this requirement. Goal 2 requires the highest minimum expected return that will be achieved 85% of the time. Sub-Portfolio C meets this requirement (and has a minimum expected return of 3.26%).

7. C is correct. A risk parity asset allocation is based on the notion that each asset class should contribute equally to the total risk of the portfolio. Bonds have the lowest risk level and must contribute 25% of the portfolio's total risk, so bonds must be overweighted (greater than 25%). The equal contribution of each asset class is calculated as:

$$w_i \times \text{Cov}(r_i, r_p) = \frac{1}{n}\sigma_p^2$$

where
w_i = weight of asset i
$\text{Cov}(r_i, r_p)$ = covariance of asset i with the portfolio
n = number of assets
σ_p^2 = variance of the portfolio

In this example, there are four asset classes, and the variance of the total portfolio is assumed to be 25%; therefore, using a risk parity approach, the allocation to each asset class is expected to contribute $(1/4 \times 25\%) = 6.25\%$ of the total variance. Because bonds have the lowest covariance, they must have a higher relative weight to achieve the same contribution to risk as the other asset classes.

8. A is correct. Comment 1 is correct because the "120 minus your age" rule reduces the equity allocation as the client ages, while the 60/40 rule makes no such adjustment. Comments 2 and 3 are not correct. The Yale model emphasizes investing in alternative assets (such as hedge funds, private equity, and real estate) as opposed to investing in traditional asset classes (such as stock and bonds). The $1/N$ rule allocates an equal weight to each asset without regard to its investment characteristics, treating all assets as indistinguishable in terms of mean returns, volatility, and correlations.

9. C is correct. The risk aversion coefficient (λ) for Mary Perkins is 8. The utility of each asset allocation is calculated as follows:

Asset Allocation A:
$U_A = 10.0\% - 0.005(8)(12\%)^2$
$\quad = 4.24\%$

Asset Allocation B:
$$U_B = 8.0\% - 0.005(8)(8\%)^2$$
$$= 5.44\%$$
Asset Allocation C:
$$U_C = 6.0\% - 0.005(8)(2\%)^2$$
$$= 5.84\%$$

Therefore, the preferred strategic allocation is Asset Allocation C, which generates the highest utility given Perkins's level of risk aversion.

10. C is correct. Less liquid asset classes—such as direct real estate, infrastructure, and private equity—represent unique challenges when applying many of the common asset allocation techniques. Common illiquid asset classes cannot be readily diversified to eliminate idiosyncratic risk, so representing overall asset class performance is problematic. Furthermore, there are far fewer indexes that attempt to represent aggregate performance for these less liquid asset classes than indexes of traditional highly liquid asset classes. Finally, the risk and return characteristics associated with actual investment vehicles— such as direct real estate funds, infrastructure funds, and private equity funds—are typically significantly different from the characteristics of the asset classes themselves.

11. B is correct. The goal of risk budgeting is to maximize return per unit of risk. A risk budget identifies the total amount of risk and attributes risk to its constituent parts. An optimum risk budget allocates risk efficiently.

12. A is correct. One common criticism of MVO is that the model outputs, the asset allocations, tend to be highly sensitive to changes in the model. Another common criticism of MVO is that the resulting asset allocations tend to be highly concentrated in a subset of the available asset classes.

13. A is correct. The factors commonly used in the factor-based approach generally have low correlations with the market and with each other. This results from the fact that the factors typically represent what is referred to as a zero (dollar) investment or self-financing investment, in which the underperforming attribute is sold short to finance an offsetting long position in the better-performing attribute. Constructing factors in this manner removes most market exposure from the factors (because of the offsetting short and long positions); as a result, the factors generally have low correlations with the market and with one another. Also, the factors commonly used in the factor-based approach are typically similar to the fundamental or structural factors used in multifactor models.

14. **Determine** which allocation in Exhibit 1 Tomb should recommend to Youngmall. (circle one)

Allocation A	Allocation B

Justify your response.
- Tomb should recommend Allocation B.
- The expected utility of Allocation B is 1.89%, which is higher than Allocation A's expected utility of 1.74%.

MVO provides a framework to determine how much to allocate to each asset class or to create the optimal asset mix. The given objective function is:

$$U_m = E(R_m) - 0.005\lambda\sigma_m^2$$

Using the given objective function and the expected returns and expected standard deviations for Allocations A and B, the expected utilities (certainty-equivalent returns) for the two allocations are calculated as:

$$\text{Allocation A: } 6.7\% - 0.005 \, (7) \, (11.9\%)^2 = 1.74\%$$

$$\text{Allocation B: } 5.9\% - 0.005 \, (7) \, (10.7\%)^2 = 1.89\%$$

Therefore, Tomb should recommend Allocation B because it results in higher expected utility than Allocation A.

15. **Contrast,** using the information provided above, the results of a reverse optimization approach with that of the MVO approach for each of the following:
    i. The asset allocation mix
       - The asset allocation weights for the reverse optimization method are inputs into the optimization and are determined by the market capitalization weights of the global market portfolio.
       - The asset allocation weights for the MVO method are outputs of the optimization with the expected returns, covariances, and a risk aversion coefficient used as inputs.
       - The two methods result in significantly different asset allocation mixes.
       - In contrast to MVO, the reverse optimization method results in a higher percentage point allocation to global bonds, US bonds, and global equities as well as a lower percentage point allocation to cash and US equities.

    The reverse optimization method takes the asset allocation weights as its inputs that are assumed to be optimal. These weights are calculated as the market capitalization weights of a global market portfolio. In contrast, the outputs of an MVO are the asset allocation weights, which are based on (1) expected returns and covariances that are forecasted using historical data and (2) a risk aversion coefficient. The two methods result in significantly different asset allocation mixes. In contrast to MVO, the reverse optimization method results in a 4.9, 5.5, and 10.1 higher percentage point allocation to US bonds, global equities, and global bonds, respectively, and a 6.1 and 14.4 lower percentage point allocation to cash and US equities, respectively.
    The asset allocation under the two methods is as follows:

		Asset Allocation Weights		
Asset Class	Market Cap (trillions)	Reverse Optimization	MVO Approach	Difference
Cash	$4.2	3.9%	10%	−6.1%
US bonds	$26.8	24.9%	20%	4.9%
US equities	$22.2	20.6%	35%	−14.4%
Global equities	$27.5	25.5%	20%	5.5%
Global bonds	$27.1	25.1%	15%	10.1%
Total	$107.8	100.0%	100.0%	

ii. The values of the expected returns for US equities and global bonds
    • For the reverse optimization approach, the expected returns of asset classes are the outputs of optimization with the market capitalization weights, covariances, and the risk aversion coefficient used as inputs.
    • In contrast, for the MVO approach, the expected returns of asset classes are inputs to the optimization, with the expected returns generally estimated using historical data.
    • The computed values for the expected returns for global bonds and US equities using the reverse optimization method are 5.3% and 9.7%, respectively.
    • In contrast, the expected return estimates used in the MVO approach from Exhibit 1 for global bonds and US equities are 4.7% and 8.6%, respectively.

The output of the reverse optimization method are optimized returns, which are viewed as unobserved equilibrium or imputed returns. The equilibrium returns are essentially long-run capital market returns provided by each asset class and are strongly linked to CAPM. In contrast, the expected returns in the MVO approach are generally forecasted based on historical data and are used as inputs along with covariances and the risk aversion coefficient in the optimization. The reverse-optimized returns are calculated using a CAPM approach. The return on an asset class using the CAPM approach is calculated as follows:

$$\text{Return on Asset Class} = \text{Risk-Free Rate} + (\text{Beta})\,(\text{Market Risk Premium})$$

Therefore, the implied returns for global bonds and US equities are calculated as follows:

$$\text{Return on Global Bonds} = 2.0\% + (0.6)\,(5.5\%) = 5.3\%$$

$$\text{Return on US Equities} = 2.0\% + (1.4)\,(5.5\%) = 9.7\%$$

Justify your response.

The implied equilibrium returns for global bonds and US equities are 5.3% and 9.7%, respectively. These implied returns are above the forecasted returns based on historical data (from Exhibit 1) used as inputs in the MVO approach for global bonds and US equities of 4.7% and 8.6%, respectively.

16. **Determine** which asset allocation in Exhibit 1 would be *most appropriate* for Johansson given her recommendation.
    (circle one)

Allocation 1	Allocation 2	Allocation 3

Justify your response.
• Allocation 3 is most appropriate.
• To fully hedge the fund's liabilities, 85% ($8.5 billion/$10.0 billion) of the fund's assets would be linked to index-linked government bonds.
• Residual $1.5 billion surplus would be invested into a return-seeking portfolio.
The pension fund currently has a surplus of $1.5 billion ($10.0 billion − $8.5 billion). To adopt a hedging/return-seeking portfolios approach, Johansson would first hedge the liabilities by allocating an amount equal to the present value of the fund's liabilities,

$8.5 billion, to a hedging portfolio. The hedging portfolio must include assets whose returns are driven by the same factors that drive the returns of the liabilities, which in this case are the index-linked government bonds.

So, Johansson should allocate 85% ($8.5 billion/$10.0 billion) of the fund's assets to index-linked government bonds. The residual $1.5 billion surplus would then be invested into a return-seeking portfolio. Therefore, Allocation 3 would be the most appropriate asset allocation for the fund because it allocates 85% of the fund's assets to index-linked government bonds and the remainder to a return-seeking portfolio consisting of corporate bonds and equities.

17. **Select**, for each of Armstrong's three goals, which sub-portfolio module from Exhibit 1 Abbott should choose in constructing a portfolio.
(circle one module for each goal)

Goal 1	Goal 2	Goal 3
Module A	Module A	Module A
Module B	Module B	Module B
Module C	Module C	Module C
Module D	Module D	Module D

Justify each selection.
- Module C should be chosen for Goal 1, Module B should be chosen for Goal 2, and Module D should be chosen for Goal 3.
- The module that should be selected for each goal is the one that offers the highest return given the time horizon and required probability of success.

The module that should be selected for each goal is the one that offers the highest return given the time horizon and required probability of success. For Goal 1, which has a time horizon of five years and a required probability of success of 85%, Module C should be chosen because its 4.4% expected return is higher than the expected returns of all the other modules. Similarly, for Goal 2, which has a time horizon of 10 years and a required probability of success of 99%, Module B should be chosen because its 2.2% expected return is higher than the expected returns of all the other modules. Finally, for Goal 3, which has a time horizon of 25 years and a required probability of success of 75%, Module D should be chosen because its 7.5% expected return is higher than the expected returns of all the other modules.

18. Guideline Answer:
- The module that should be selected for each goal is the one that offers the highest return given the time horizon and required probability of success.
- Approximately 16.4%, 12.7%, 50.4%, and 20.5% should be invested in Modules A, B, C, and D, respectively.

The appropriate goals-based allocation for the Armstrongs is as follows:

	Goals			
	1	**2**	**3**	**Surplus**
Horizon (years)	5	10	25	
Probability of success	85%	99%	75%	
Selected module	**C**	**B**	**D**	**A**
Discount rate	4.4%	2.2%	7.5%	
Dollars invested (millions)	$4.03	$1.01	$1.64	$1.32
As a % of total	**50.4%**	**12.7%**	**20.5%**	**16.4%**

Supporting calculations:

For Goal 1, which has a time horizon of five years and a required probability of success of 85%, Module C should be chosen because its 4.4% expected return is higher than the expected returns of all the other modules. The present value of Goal 1 is calculated as follows:

$$N = 5, \ FV = -5{,}000{,}000, \ I/Y = 4.4\%; \ CPT \ PV = \$4{,}031{,}508 \ (or \ \$4.03 \ million)$$

So, approximately 50.4% of the total assets of $8 million (= $4.03 million/ $8.00 million) should be allocated to Module C.

For Goal 2, which has a time horizon of 10 years and a required probability of success of 99%, Module B should be chosen because its 2.2% expected return is higher than the expected returns of all the other modules. The present value of Goal 2 is calculated as follows:

$$PV = \frac{\$100{,}000}{(1.022)^1} + \frac{\$100{,}000(1.03)^1}{(1.022)^2} + \frac{\$100{,}000(1.03)^2}{(1.022)^3} + \cdots + \frac{\$100{,}000(1.03)^9}{(1.022)^{10}}$$

$$PV = \$1{,}013{,}670 \ (or \ \$1.01 \ million)$$

So, approximately 12.7% of the total assets of $8 million (= $1.01 million/ $8.00 million) should be allocated to Module B.

For Goal 3, which has a time horizon of 25 years and a required probability of success of 75%, Module D should be chosen because its 7.5% expected return is higher than the expected returns of all the other modules. The present value of Goal 3 is calculated as follows:

$$N = 25, \ PV = -10{,}000{,}000, \ I/Y = 7.5\%; \ CPT \ PV = \$1{,}639{,}791 \ (or \ \$1.64 \ million)$$

So, approximately 20.5% of the total assets of $8 million (= $1.64 million/ $8.00 million) should be allocated to Module D.

Finally, the surplus of $1,315,032 (= $8,000,000 − $4,031,508 − $1,013,670 − $1,639,791), representing 16.4% (= $1.32 million/$8.00 million), should be invested in Module A following Abbott's suggestion.

CHAPTER 7

ASSET ALLOCATION WITH REAL-WORLD CONSTRAINTS

SOLUTIONS

1. A is correct. A lower annual spending rate, in addition to the board's expectations of rising enrollment and minimal need for endowment support over the next five years, indicates a decreased need for liquidity. Therefore, KUE could justify an increase in the strategic allocation to less liquid asset classes (such as private real estate equity and infrastructure) and a decrease in the strategic allocation to liquid assets (such as investment-grade bonds).

2. A is correct. The Sharpe ratio is suitable for measuring the success of TAA relative to SAA. Specifically, the success of TAA decisions can be evaluated by comparing the Sharpe ratio realized under the TAA with the Sharpe ratio that would have been realized under the SAA.

3. A is correct. The forecast for expected excess returns is positive for developed markets equity and negative for infrastructure. Therefore, to attempt to profit from the short-term excess return forecast, KUE can overweight developed markets equity and underweight infrastructure. These adjustments to the asset-class weights are within KUE's lower and upper policy limits.

4. C is correct. As a general rule, the portion of a taxable asset owner's assets that are eligible for lower tax rates and deferred capital gains tax treatment should first be allocated to the investor's taxable accounts. Assets that generate returns mainly from interest income tend to be less tax efficient and in Koval's country are taxed at progressively higher rates. Also, the standard deviation (volatility) of after-tax returns is lower when equities are held in a taxable account. Therefore, Koval's taxable account would become more tax efficient if it held more domestic equities focused on long-term capital gain opportunities.

5. B is correct. Availability bias is an information-processing bias in which people take a mental shortcut when estimating the probability of an outcome based on how easily the outcome comes to mind. On the basis of the losses incurred by his family trust during

129

the recent economic crisis, Koval expresses a strong preference for avoiding the emerging markets equity asset class. Such behavior is consistent with availability bias, where investors who personally experience an adverse event are likely to assign a higher probability to such an event occurring again.

6. B is correct. After-tax portfolio optimization requires adjusting each asset class's expected return and risk for expected taxes. The correlation of returns is not affected by taxes and does not require an adjustment when performing after-tax portfolio optimization.

7. A is correct. The changing character of liabilities through time affects the asset allocation to fund those liabilities. The Martins' investment horizon for some of their assets has changed. The amount of liquidity needed for Lara's near-term education has been greatly reduced owing to the receipt of the scholarship. The Martins will likely still have to pay for some university-related expenses; however, a large part of the $120,000 in cash that is earmarked for Lara's expenses can now be allocated to the Martins' long-term goal of early retirement. Retirement is 18 years away, much longer than the one- to five-year horizon for university expenses. Therefore, the Martins' allocation to cash would likely decrease.

8. C is correct. The Martins' sub-portfolio is aspirational and a low priority. Investors are usually willing to take more risk on lower-priority, aspirational portfolios. The charitable gift will be made from their estate, which indicates a long time horizon. In addition, the Martins want the highest return possible. Therefore, the highest allocation to equities is most appropriate.

9. A is correct. Taxes alter the distribution of returns by both reducing the expected mean return and muting the dispersion of returns. The portion of an owner's taxable assets that are eligible for lower tax rates and deferred capital gains tax treatment should first be allocated to the investor's taxable accounts.

10. A is correct. The Martins wish to maintain the same risk level for both retirement accounts based on their strategic asset allocation. However, more frequent rebalancing exposes the taxable asset owner to realized taxes that could have otherwise been deferred or even avoided. Rebalancing is discretionary, and the Martins also wish to minimize taxes. Because after-tax return volatility is lower than pre-tax return volatility, it takes larger asset-class movements to materially alter the risk profile of a taxable portfolio. This suggests that rebalancing ranges for a taxable portfolio can be wider than those of a tax-exempt/tax-deferred portfolio with a similar risk profile; thus, rebalancing occurs less frequently.

11. C is correct. Representativeness, or recency, bias is the tendency to overweight the importance of the most recent observations and information relative to a longer-dated or more comprehensive set of long-term observations and information. Return chasing is a common result of this bias, and it results in overweighting asset classes with strong recent performance.

12. A is correct. McCall recommends a new IPS. Changes in the economic environment and capital market expectations or changes in the beliefs of committee members are factors that may lead to an altering of the principles that guide investment activities. Because the plan is now overfunded, there is less need to take a higher level of equity risk. The Pension Committee is concerned about the impact of future market and economic risks on the funding status of the plan. Katt Company operates in a cyclical industry and could have difficulty making pension contributions during a recession.

Therefore, a substantial reduction in the allocation to stocks and an increase in bonds reduce risk. The 40% stocks/60% bonds alternative increases the allocation to bonds from 35% to 60%. Increasing the fixed-income allocation should moderate plan risk, provide a better hedge for liabilities, and reduce contribution uncertainty.

13. B is correct. Using rules-based, quantitative signals, systematic tactical asset allocation (TAA) attempts to capture asset-class-level return anomalies that have been shown to have some predictability and persistence. Trend signals are widely used in systematic TAA. A moving-average crossover is a trend signal that indicates an upward (downward) trend when the moving average of the shorter time frame, 50 days, is above (below) the moving average of the longer time frame, 200 days.

14. Of the six potential behavioral biases, Young is most likely exhibiting three as explained below.

Identify the behavioral biases Young is *most likely* exhibiting. (Circle the correct answers.)
Justify each response.

Bias	Justification
Loss Aversion	Under loss-aversion bias, people strongly prefer avoiding losses as opposed to achieving gains and they assign a greater weight to potential negative outcomes than positive ones. Young's strong emphasis on retirement security and her desire to avoid losing money indicates that she has a loss-aversion bias. This bias could interfere with her willingness to maintain ideal asset allocations during times of negative returns.
Illusion of Control	
Mental Accounting	Under mental accounting bias, people treat one sum of money differently from another sum based solely on the mental account to which the money is assigned. Young is considering her $3 million tax-deferred retirement account, her $500,000 account for the girls' education, and the $400,000 emergency account separately, rather than seeing them all as a combined investable total. In doing this, she sets herself up for the possibility of sub-optimal allocation.
Representative Bias	
Framing Bias	
Availability Bias	Under availability bias, people take a mental shortcut when estimating the probability of an outcome based on how easily the outcome comes to mind. Easily recalled outcomes are often perceived as being more likely than those that are harder to recall or understand. Young's strong emphasis on retirement security and her desire to avoid losing money both could be driven by her strong memories of her childhood financial hardships.

15. **Determine** which proposed portfolio *most closely* meets Young's desired objectives. (Circle one.)

Portfolio 1	Portfolio 2	Portfolio 3

Justify your response.

Portfolio 3 comes closest to meeting Young's desire to earn at least 6% after tax per year without taking on additional incremental risk. Portfolio 3 offers a lower standard deviation than Portfolio 2, as summarized in Exhibit 3, while producing approximately the same return. Portfolio 1 achieves the highest returns but at a much greater level of volatility than Portfolio 3, not satisfying Young's risk criterion.

Given the $500,000 minimum investment requirement for alternative assets, at Young's total portfolio size of $5.5 million, the suggested 5% allocation to private equity in Portfolio 2 results in only a $275,000 exposure, insufficient to invest in private equity. Thus, Portfolio 2, as presented, is not viable, whereas Portfolio 1, with a private equity investment of $550,000, meets the minimum requirement for alternative investments. This minimum investment requirement is not an issue for Portfolio 3 because it has no private equity component.

Asset Class	Portfolio 3	Pre-Tax Return	Post-Tax Return	Resulting Return
Municipal Bonds	30%	3%	3.00%	0.90%
Small-Cap Equities	35%	12%	9.00%	3.15%
Large-Cap Equities	35%	10%	7.50%	2.63%
Private Equity	0%	25%	18.75%	0.00%
Total	100%			6.68%

Asset Class	Portfolio 1	Pre-Tax Return	Post-Tax Return	Resulting Return
Municipal Bonds	5%	3%	3.00%	0.15%
Small-Cap Equities	50%	12%	9.00%	4.50%
Large-Cap Equities	35%	10%	7.50%	2.63%
Private Equity	10%	25%	18.75%	1.88%
Total	100%			9.15%

Asset Class	Portfolio 2	Pre-Tax Return	Post-Tax Return	Resulting Return
Municipal Bonds	35%	3%	3.00%	1.05%
Small-Cap Equities	10%	12%	9.00%	0.90%
Large-Cap Equities	50%	10%	7.50%	3.75%
Private Equity	5%	25%	18.75%	0.94%
Total	100%			6.64%

16.   **Determine** which alternative (circle one) *best* fits each account.

Account	Alternative	**Justify** each selection.
$5.5 Million Account	Alternative 1 Alternative 2	The $5.5 million account is after tax. Because after-tax volatility is lower than pre-tax volatility, the rebalancing range for an after-tax account is wider. The range reflected for Alternative 2 is 10.7%, whereas the range for Alternative 1 is 8.0% (to achieve the same risk constraint), reflecting the impact of taxes on the $5.5 million account. In addition, asset sales in the after-tax account result in taxes due. A wider target range allows more price movement before the rebalancing range is exceeded (and a decision must be made to initiate an asset sale, incur associated tax payments, and rebalance back to the target equity allocation). The after-tax account range is calculated by adjusting the pre-tax range for taxes. After-tax rebalancing range = Pre-tax rebalancing range/(1 − Tax rate). 8.0%/(1 − 0.25) 10.67%
$3.0 Million Account	Alternative 1 Alternative 2	The $3.0 million is a tax-deferred retirement account. Because pre-tax volatility is higher than after-tax volatility, the rebalancing range for a pre-tax account is narrower. The range reflected for Alternative 1 is 8.0%, whereas the range for Alternative 2 is 10.7% (to achieve the same risk constraint), reflecting the impact of tax deferral on the $3.0 million account versus the effect of taxes on the $5.5 million account.

17. **Identify** the *primary* reason for the broker's reassessment of Young's circumstances. (Circle one.)

Change in goals	**Change in constraints**	**Change in beliefs**

Justify your response.

A change in constraints relates to material changes in constraints, such as time horizon, liquidity needs, asset size, and regulatory or other external constraints. In this case, Young's circumstances have changed; she is considering accepting the offer and retiring five years sooner than she originally anticipated.

A change in an investor's personal circumstances that may alter her risk appetite or risk capacity is considered to be a change in *goals*. In this circumstance, Young's risk appetite or risk capacity have not changed, whereas the time horizon associated with her goals has.

A change in the investment beliefs or principles guiding an investor's investment activities is considered to be a change in *beliefs*. In this circumstance, Young's guiding principles have not changed.

Young decides to accept the retirement offer. Having very low liquidity needs, she wants to save part of the retirement payout for unforeseen costs that might occur more than a decade in the future. The broker's view on long-term stock market prospects is positive and recommends additional equity investment.

18. **Determine** which of Young's accounts is *best* suited for implementing the broker's recommendation. (Circle one.)

Account	Justification
Education	
Reallocated Money Market	As a general rule, the portion of a taxable asset owner's assets that is eligible for lower tax rates and deferred capital gains tax treatment should first be allocated to the investor's taxable accounts. Equities should generally be held in taxable accounts, whereas taxable bonds and high turnover trading strategies should generally be located in tax-exempt and tax-deferred accounts.
	The reallocated money market account is a taxable account, whereas the retirement account is tax-deferred. The unexpected needs account requires liquidity (in case of unexpected needs), so it is better suited for shorter-term positions.
	Given the ages of Young's two daughters, now 17 and 20, the education account is most likely currently funding college expenses and will be for the next several years. Accordingly, it needs to be invested in highly liquid assets to cover these costs.
Retirement	
Unexpected Needs	

19. The proposed asset allocation for Titan is not appropriate because:
    1. Given the shift in enrollment trends and declining donations resulting from the sanctions, Titan will likely need greater liquidity in the future because of the increased probability of higher outflows to support university operations. The proposed asset allocation shifts Titan's allocation into risky assets (increases the relative equity holdings and decreases the relative bond holdings), which would introduce greater uncertainty as to their future value.
    2. Titan is relatively small for the proposed addition of private equity. Access to such an asset class as private equity may be constrained for smaller asset owners, such as Titan, who may lack the related internal investment expertise. Additionally, the Sun-Fin Private Equity Fund minimum investment level is $1 million. This level of investment in private equity would be 10% of Titan's total portfolio value. Given Titan's declining financial position due to declining enrollments and its resulting potential need for liquidity, private equity at this minimum level of investment is not appropriate for Titan.

20. The proposed asset allocation for Fordhart is inappropriate because:
    1. Given the increasing enrollment trends and recent favorable legal settlement, Fordhart will likely require lower liquidity in the future. The proposed allocation shifts Fordhart's portfolio away from risky assets (decreases the relative equity holdings and increases the relative bond holdings).
    2. The proposed 10% allocation to private equity creates an overly concentrated position in the underlying investment. A 10% allocation to the CFQ Private Equity Fund is $200 million (10% of Fordhart's $2 billion). The CFQ Private Equity Fund has assets under management (AUM) of $500 million. Hence, Fordhart would own 40% of the entire CFQ Private Equity Fund. This position exposes both Fordhart and the CFQ fund to an undesirable level of operational risk.

CHAPTER 8

ASSET ALLOCATION TO ALTERNATIVE INVESTMENTS

SOLUTIONS

1. C is correct. Real assets (which include energy, infrastructure, timber, commodities, and farmland) are generally believed to mitigate the risks to the portfolio arising from unexpected inflation. Commodities act as a hedge against a core constituent of inflation measures. Rather than investing directly in the actual commodities, commodity futures may be incorporated using a managed futures strategy. In addition, the committee is looking for an asset class that has a low correlation with public equities, which will provide diversification benefits. Commodities are regarded as having much lower correlation coefficients with public equities than with private equities and hedge funds. Therefore, commodities will provide the greatest potential to fulfill the indicated role and to diversify public equities.

2. C is correct. When projecting expected returns, the order of returns from highest to lowest is typically regarded as private equities, hedge funds, bonds. Therefore, the probability of achieving the highest portfolio return while maintaining the funded status of the plan would require the use of private equities in conjunction with public equities. In addition, private equities have a high/strong potential to fulfill the role of capital growth. Fixed-income investments are expected to have a high/strong potential to fulfill the role of safety.

3. B is correct. A traditional approach has been used to define the opportunity set based on different macroeconomic conditions. The primary limitations of traditional approaches are that they overestimate the portfolio diversification and obscure the primary drivers of risk.

4. C is correct. With the introduction of the early retirement incentive plan (ERIP), the defined benefit pension plan will likely be called upon to make pension payments earlier than originally scheduled. As a result, the near term liquidity of the plan is the greatest risk arising from the addition of the alternative asset classes (e.g., private equities, hedge funds, and real estate). Investments in alternatives, such as private equities, can take

upwards of five years to reach a full commitment and potentially another decade to unwind.

5. B is correct. The pension plan's investment in private equities via a blind pool presents the prospect that less than perfect transparency will be associated with the underlying holdings of the alternative asset manager. Capital is committed for an investment in a portfolio of assets that are not specified in advance. In addition, reporting for alternative funds is often less transparent than investors are accustomed to seeing on their stock and bond portfolios.

6. C is correct. Statement 3 is correct because risk factor-based approaches to asset allocation can be applied to develop more robust asset allocations. Statement 4 is correct because a mean–variance optimization typically overallocates to the private alternative asset classes, partly because of underestimated risk due to stale pricing and the assumption that returns are normally distributed

7. C is correct. Park notes that the current macroeconomic environment could lead to a bear market within a few years. Liquidity planning should take into account that under a scenario in which public equities and fixed-income investments are expected to perform poorly, general partners may exercise an option to extend the life of the fund.

8. A is correct. Fund A should be selected based on both quantitative and qualitative factors. Fund A has a five-year IRR (12.9%) that is slightly lower than, but comparable to, both Fund B (13.2%) and Fund C (13.1%). Given the sensitivity to the timing of cash flows into and out of a fund associated with the IRR calculation, however, the final decision should not be based merely on quantitative returns. It is also important to monitor the investment process and the investment management firm itself, particularly in alternative investment structures. Considering the qualitative factors identified by Park, Fund A is the only fund with a strong, positive factor: It benefits from service providers (administrators, custodians, and auditors) with impeccable reputations. Fund B seems to be experiencing style drift, which suggests that the returns are not consistent with the manager's advertised investment edge (hence, a negative factor). Fund C has experienced the departure of key persons, which puts future fund returns in jeopardy (hence, a negative factor).

9. C is correct. An absolute return hedge fund has a greater potential to diversify the fund's dominant public equity risk than either private equity or private real estate. Absolute return hedge funds exhibit an equity beta that is often less than that of private equity or private real estate. Also, absolute return hedge funds tend to exhibit a high potential to diversify public equities, whereas equity long/short hedge funds exhibit a moderate potential to fulfill this role.

A is incorrect because although private equity provides moderate diversification against public equity, an absolute return hedge fund has a greater potential to do so. The primary advantage of private equity is capital growth.

B is incorrect because private real estate provides only moderate diversification against public equity, whereas absolute return hedge funds have a greater potential to do so. The primary advantage of private real estate is income generation.

10. B is correct. While bonds reduce the probability of achieving a target return over time, they have been more effective as a volatility mitigator than alternatives over an extended period of time.

A is incorrect because Statement 1 is correct. Short-biased strategies are expected to provide some measure of alpha in addition to lowering a portfolio's overall equity beta.

C is incorrect because Statement 3 is correct. Short-biased equity strategies help reduce an equity-dominated portfolio's overall beta. Short-biased strategies are believed to deliver equity-like returns with less-than-full exposure to the equity premium but with an additional source of return that might come from the manager's shorting of individual stocks.

11. A is correct. Among the three portfolios, Portfolio A minimizes the probability of triggering the primary lender's loan covenant, which is the highest-priority goal, because it has the lowest one-year 99% CVaR, −19.4%. Portfolio A also has the lowest probability of purchasing power impairment over a 10-year horizon (2.5%). While Portfolio A has the lowest probability of achieving a real return target of 6% over a 10-year horizon (56.1%), that is the least important goal to be met. Therefore, Gension should recommend Portfolio A for the fund.

    B is incorrect because Portfolio B has a one-year 99% CVaR of −20.6%, which crosses the loan covenant threshold of a 20% loss. Portfolio A is the only one that satisfies the most important goal and is the portfolio least likely to trigger the loan covenant. Since Portfolio B does not achieve the most important goal of minimizing the probability of triggering the primary lender's loan covenant, Portfolio B should not be the recommended portfolio.

    C is incorrect because despite the fact that Portfolio C has the highest probability of meeting the 6% real return over a 10-year horizon, 61.0%, it also has a one-year 99% CVaR of −22.7% and thus the highest probability of triggering the loan covenant. Portfolio A is the only one that satisfies the most important goal and is the portfolio least likely to trigger the loan covenant. Since Portfolio C does not achieve the most important goal of minimizing the probability of triggering the primary lender's loan covenant, Portfolio C should not be the recommended portfolio.

12. B is correct. As a public pension fund that is required to provide detailed reports to the public, a primary concern for the IC is transparency. Investors in alternative investments must be comfortable with less than 100% transparency in their holdings. Private equity funds often necessitate buying into a "blind pool." Although an investor can look at the assets acquired in a manager's previous funds, there is no assurance that future investments will exactly replicate the previous funds.

    A is incorrect because the IC has a formal investment policy, as well as an in-house team with experience in alternatives and the knowledge and capacity to critically evaluate alternative investments.

    C is incorrect because the IC has a long-term investment horizon. While investors with less than a 15-year horizon should generally avoid investing in alternatives, the IC has a 20-year investment horizon that should easily accommodate an investment in private equity.

13. A is correct. REITs are most appropriate for funds committed to private real estate investments since they will have the most similar return and risk characteristics and will help maintain the strategic asset allocation of the plan. Although cash equivalents have less volatility over a short-term horizon, they are less likely to meet the plan's long-term return objectives.

    B is incorrect because the opportunity cost of being out of the markets over the next few years during the capital call period makes cash equivalents an inappropriate investment. Although cash equivalents have lower volatility, which is often desirable over a short-term period, they will not help the plan meet its long-term return objectives.

C is incorrect because, although REITs will have the return and risk characteristics most similar to private real estate, a 20% allocation is not large enough to achieve the plan's long-term return objectives. The 80% allocation to cash equivalents will greatly affect the return, making the plan less likely to meet the long-term return objectives.

14. **Determine** which asset class is *most likely* to meet Pua's investment objective. (Circle one.)

Determine which asset class is *most likely* to meet Pua's investment objective. (Circle one.)	**Justify** your response.
Public Real Estate	• Timber exhibits a low correlation with public equities and can fulfill the functional role of risk diversification. • Timber provides high long-term returns and can fulfill the functional role of capital growth.
Private Real Assets (Timber)	Private real assets (timber) is the asset class most likely to meet Pua's objective. Private real assets, such as timber, tend to exhibit a low correlation with public equities and therefore have a high potential to fulfill the functional role of risk diversification in Pua's current all-equity portfolio. In addition, timber has a high potential to fulfill the functional role of capital growth in the portfolio since growth is provided by the underlying biological growth of the tree as well as through appreciation in the underlying land value.
Equity Long/Short Hedge Funds	Compared with timber, public real estate as an asset class would likely offer less opportunity for capital growth and lower diversification benefits. Also, equity long/short hedge funds as an asset class would provide a moderate degree of risk diversification in Pua's all-equity portfolio but do not carry significant capital growth potential.

15. • Pua's investment has been affected by key person risk as shown by the effect of the management change.
   • Style drift has occurred as shown by the change from a local to a regional investment strategy and the expansion of the investment strategy to include commercial properties.
   • The risk of the investment has changed owing to the added complexity of the property renovations.
   • The longer holding periods and the change in interim profit distribution targets will affect this investment.
   • Client/asset turnover following the management change may now affect the performance of the investment.
   • The management change may alter the client profile, which could have a negative effect on investment performance.

Qualitative considerations can lead to a better understanding of the revised strategy for the investment and whether this investment remains suitable for Pua. Pua's investment has been affected by key person risk as shown by the management change from the local manager to a national company. Style drift has occurred as shown by the change from a local to a regional investment strategy and the expansion of the strategy to include commercial properties.

The risk of the investment has changed because of the added complexity of the renovations, and monitoring the company's risk management will be important for Greslö as she manages Pua's portfolio. Monitoring of the private real estate investment has revealed discrepancies in the new management strategy of the national company relative to the initial investment strategy of the local manager, including the longer holding periods and the changed interim profit distribution targets. Client/asset turnover following the management change may now significantly affect the performance of the investment. Finally, the change in management may alter the client profile, which could have a negative effect on investment performance.

16. **Determine** which of the potential investment vehicles *best* meets the investment considerations for Ælfheah. (Circle one.)

	Justify your response.	**Explain** for *each* investment not selected why the investment considerations are not met.
Publicly traded US REIT	The publicly traded US REIT offers tax advantages to Ælfheah from the depreciation of its US real estate assets. The depreciation would help offset income received on those assets. In addition, the REIT would not require an in-house management team; thus, Ælfheah can maintain low overhead costs.	
Relative value hedge fund		The relative value hedge fund is unlikely to be a tax-efficient strategy for Ælfheah. This tax inefficiency is seen frequently with many hedge fund strategies, especially those funds and fund companies where tax-exempt investors dominate the client base. The fund manager may be insensitive to tax considerations for a taxable investor such as Ælfheah.
Tax-efficient angel investment		The tax-efficient angel investment is a specialized investment that will require a highly customized investment approach. Researching and managing this type of investment will require an in-house team to locate and supervise these more specialized investments. Adding these resources would increase overhead costs and violate the IC's investment consideration of maintaining low overhead costs.

17. **Determine** which approach to determine the asset allocation is *most appropriate* for Ælfheah. (Circle one.)   **Justify** your response.

Traditional

- The traditional approach is more appropriate since describing the roles of various asset classes is intuitive.
- This approach will be easier for Ng to explain to the IC, whose members have only a basic understanding of the investment process.
- This approach will make it easier to identify relevant mandates for the portfolio's alternative investments.
- Since Ælfheah seeks to maintain low overhead costs, the risk-based approach would not be appropriate.

Risk based

The traditional approach is more appropriate for Ælfheah. The IC is less sophisticated in its understanding of alternative investments but may have some familiarity with the traditional asset class-based approach. Listing the roles of various asset classes will be more intuitive and easy for Ng to explain to the IC.

The traditional approach has relevance for the IC's liquidity and operational considerations. This approach will make it easier to identify relevant mandates for the alternative investments in the portfolio. The traditional approach also will allow the IC to obtain a better understanding of how various asset classes behave so that Ng can tailor the asset allocation to address any concerns. The traditional approach will be easier to implement, and the IC does not want to add costly in-house resources, which would likely be necessary with the risk-based approach.

18. **Determine** the investment vehicle that would be *most appropriate* for Ælfheah's proposed alternative asset class. (Circle one.)

	Justify your response.
FOFs	• An FOF would allow Ælfheah to co-invest with other investors in alternative investment opportunities for which Ælfheah might otherwise be too small to participate. • An in-house team would not be necessary to review and maintain an FOF, which uses an outside manager. • Ælfheah is unlikely to meet the very high minimum investment of an SMA, which may also require enhanced in-house investment resources. • Ælfheah does not need the higher liquidity of UCITS, which have a less attractive risk/return profile for Ælfheah's relatively small-sized portfolio.
SMAs	An FOF is the most appropriate investment vehicle for Ælfheah. This vehicle allows Ælfheah to co-invest alongside other investors in order to participate in alternative investment opportunities for which it would otherwise be too small to participate. An expert in-house team would not be necessary to review and maintain the types of investments in an FOF since this investment vehicle uses an outside manager.
UCITS	SMAs are available for certain large portfolios, such as those of large family offices or foundations, but it is unlikely that Ælfheah would meet the very high minimum investment requirement. This type of investment poses greater operational challenges for the investor; thus, an SMA may require enhanced in-house investment resources. UCITS are less appropriate for Ælfheah since the pension plan is a medium-sized (not small-sized) investor and its liquidity needs are being met. Ælfheah should instead invest in a vehicle that offers lower liquidity with a more attractive risk/return profile. Also, UCITS have regulatory restrictions that can make them more difficult for a fund manager to implement the desired investment strategy.

19. **Determine** the asset allocation approach that is *most suitable* for the Endowment. (Circle one.)

Justify your response.

MVO	• Mean–CVaR will better address the IC's concern about left-tail risk (the risk of a permanent capital loss).
	• If the portfolio contains asset classes and investment strategies with negative skewness and long tails, CVaR optimization could materially alter the asset allocation decision.
Mean–CVaR optimization	Given the IC's investment objectives for the endowment, using a mean–CVaR optimization approach is more suitable for determining the asset allocation. The IC has 36% of its portfolio invested in alternative assets, 19% in private equity, and 17% in hedge funds. Thus, the IC has a more sophisticated understanding of risk and will appreciate the more nuanced view of risk offered by mean–CVaR optimization. The portfolio has exposure to alternative investments, and the IC is concerned about left-tail risk (the risk of a permanent loss of capital), as indicated to Calixto. Thus, the asset allocation decision will be enhanced by the more detailed understanding of left-tail risk offered by mean–CVaR optimization relative to MVO. MVO cannot easily accommodate the characteristics of most alternative investments. MVO characterizes an asset's risk using standard deviation. Standard deviation, a one-dimensional view of risk, is a poor representation of the risk characteristics of alternative investments for which asset returns may be not normally distributed. MVO typically over-allocates to alternative asset classes, partly because risk is underestimated because of stale or infrequent pricing and the underlying assumption that returns are normally distributed. An investor particularly concerned with the downside risk of a proposed asset allocation may choose to minimize the portfolio's CVaR rather than its volatility relative to a return target. If the portfolio contains asset classes and investment strategies with negative skewness and long tails, CVaR optimization could materially alter the asset allocation decision.

20. The expected NAV of the fund at the end of the current year is €25,258,050, calculated as follows:

    First, the expected distribution at the end of the current year is calculated as

    Expected distribution = [Prior-year NAV × (1 + Growth rate)] × (Distribution rate).

    Expected distribution = [(€25,000,000 × 1.11) × 18%] = €4,995,000.

    Therefore, the expected NAV of the fund at the end of the current year is

    Expected NAV = [Prior-year NAV × (1 + Growth rate) + Capital contributions − Distributions)] × (1 + Growth rate).

    Expected NAV = [(€25,000,000 × 1.11) + 0 − €4,995,000] × 1.11
                 = €25,258,050.

EXCHANGE-TRADED FUNDS: MECHANICS AND APPLICATIONS

SOLUTIONS

1. B is correct. ETFs trade in both primary and secondary markets. The primary market for ETF trading is that which exists on an over-the-counter basis between authorized participants (APs), a special group of institutional investors, and the ETF issuer or sponsor. This process is referred to as creation/redemption, and it is only through these primary market transactions that shares of the ETF can be created or destroyed. ETFs also trade in the secondary market on exchanges. Secondary market trading happens between any pair of market participants—individual or institutional investors, market makers, and so on.

2. B is correct. Each day, ETF managers publicly disclose a list of securities that they want to own, which is referred to as the creation basket. This basket also serves as the portfolio for determining the intrinsic net asset value (NAV) of the ETF on the basis of prices during the trading day.

3. B is correct. The AP generally absorbs all the costs associated with buying or selling the securities in the baskets or the ETF shares and pays an additional fee to the ETF provider to cover processing fees associated with creation/redemption activities. APs pass these costs to investors in the ETF's bid–ask spread, which is incurred by investors entering (ETF share buyers) and exiting (ETF share sellers) the fund.

4. A is correct. When the share price of an ETF is trading at a premium to its intraday NAV and assuming arbitrage costs are minimal, APs will step in and take advantage of the arbitrage. Specifically, APs will step in and buy the basket of securities that the ETF tracks (the creation basket) and exchange it with the ETF provider for new ETF shares (a creation unit). These new shares received by APs can then be sold on the open market to realize arbitrage profits.

5. C is correct. An ETF's tracking error is typically reported as the annualized standard deviation of the daily differential returns of the ETF and its benchmark.

6. B is correct. A rolling return assessment, referred to in the ETF industry as the "tracking difference," provides a more informative picture of the investment outcome for an investor in an ETF. Such an analysis allows investors to see the cumulative effect of portfolio management and expenses over an extended period. It also allows for comparison with other annual metrics such as a fund's expense ratio. Tracking error, as a statistic, reveals only ETF tracking variability; it does not reveal to investors whether the fund is over- or underperforming its index or whether that tracking error is concentrated over a few days or is more consistently experienced. An ETF's expense ratio does not fully reflect the investor experience. That is, the expense ratio does not reflect the cost of portfolio rebalancing or other fees, making it an inferior assessment measure relative to a rolling return assessment.

7. B is correct. An ETF's tracking error is typically reported as the annualized standard deviation of the daily differential returns of the ETF and its benchmark. Therefore, an ETF's reported tracking error indicates to investors the magnitude by which an ETF's returns deviate from those of its benchmark over time.

8. C is correct. Although additions and deletions of securities from the underlying benchmark index may occur and result in tracking error, such index changes generally occur infrequently (often quarterly). In addition, ETF portfolio managers may work with APs for index rebalance trades to ensure market-on-close pricing to minimize this source of tracking error. Therefore, the resulting tracking error caused by index changes will not likely be as large as the tracking error caused by representative sampling or by fees and expenses incurred by the ETF.

9. A is correct. ETFs tend to distribute far less in capital gains relative to mutual funds. This is mostly due to the fact that ETFs have historically had significantly lower turnover than mutual funds have had.

10. A is correct. Return-of-capital distributions are amounts paid out in excess of an ETF's earnings and serve to reduce an investor's cost basis by the amount of the distribution. These distributions are generally not taxable.

11. A is correct. Fund-closure risk is the risk that an ETF may shut down. The reasons that lead to an ETF closing down often have to do with changes in regulations, increased competition, and corporate activity (merger and acquisition activity within the ETF industry).

12. C is correct. Expectation-related risk is the risk that some ETF investors may not fully understand how more complex ETFs will perform because of a lack of understanding of sophisticated asset classes and strategies.

13. C is correct. ETF trading costs in the form of commissions and bid–ask spreads are paid by investors buying or selling ETF shares on an exchange. These trading costs are influenced by the bid–ask spread of the ETF, the size of the trade relative to the normal trading activity of the ETF, and the ease of hedging the ETF by the market-making community. Even the closing price of the ETF on the exchange includes a premium or discount to the NAV, driven by supply and demand factors on the exchange and the market impact costs of executing an exchange transaction. The purchase and sale trading costs of an ETF are paid regardless of holding period, whereas other costs, such as management fees, increase as the holding period lengthens.

14. A is correct. The expected total holding-period cost for investing in the ETF over a nine-month holding period is calculated as follows:

Total holding-period cost = Annual management fee + Round-trip trading commissions + Bid–offer spread on purchase/sale.

Total holding-period cost = (9/12) × (0.40%) + 0.55% + 0.20% = 1.05%.

15. B is correct. ETF bid–ask spreads are generally less than or equal to the combination of the following:
    - ± Creation/redemption fees and other direct costs, such as brokerage and exchange fees
    - + Bid–ask spread of the underlying securities held by the ETF
    - + Compensation for the risk of hedging or carrying positions by liquidity providers (market makers) for the remainder of the trading day
    - + Market maker's desired profit spread
    - −Discount related to the likelihood of receiving an offsetting ETF order in a short time frame

    For very liquid and high-volume ETFs, buyers and sellers are active throughout the trading day. Therefore, because most of these ETF trades are matched extremely quickly and never involve the creation/redemption process, the first three factors listed do not contribute heavily to their bid–ask spreads. So, creation/redemption fees and other direct costs are not likely to have much influence on these ETFs' bid–ask spreads.

16. B is correct. Factor strategy ETFs are usually benchmarked to an index created with predefined rules for screening and/or weighting stock holdings and are considered longer-term, buy-and-hold investment options rather than tactical trading instruments. The strategy index rules are structured around return drivers or factors, such as value, dividend yield, earnings or dividend growth, quality, stock volatility, or momentum. Investors using factor-based investing seek outperformance versus a benchmark or portfolio risk modification.

17. C is correct. ETFs that have the highest trading volumes in their asset class category are generally preferred for tactical trading applications.

18. B is correct. Statement 2 is correct. A significant advantage of the ETF creation/ redemption process is that the AP absorbs all costs of transacting the securities for the fund's portfolio. APs pass these costs to investors in the ETF's bid–ask spread, incurred by ETF buyers and sellers. Thus, non-transacting shareholders of an ETF are shielded from the negative impact of transaction costs caused by other investors entering and exiting the fund. In contrast, when investors enter or exit a traditional mutual fund, the mutual fund manager incurs costs to buy or sell investments arising from this activity, which affects all fund shareholders. This makes the ETF structure inherently fairer: Frequent ETF traders bear the cost of their activity, while buy-and-hold ETF shareholders are shielded from those costs. Investors cannot short mutual fund shares, but they can short ETF shares. Also, if ETF shares are trading at a discount to NAV and arbitrage costs are sufficiently low, APs will buy ETF shares and exchange them for the securities in the redemption basket. Statement 3 describes the scenario that would occur if the ETF shares are trading at a premium to NAV.

    A is incorrect because Statement 1 is incorrect. Investors cannot short mutual fund shares, but they can short ETF shares.

C is incorrect because Statement 3 is incorrect. If ETF shares are trading at a discount to NAV and arbitrage costs are sufficiently low, APs will buy ETF shares and exchange them for the securities in the redemption basket. Statement 3 describes the scenario that would occur if ETF shares are trading at a premium to NAV.

19. A is correct. When the share price of an ETF is trading at a premium to its intraday NAV and arbitrage costs are minimal, APs will step in and take advantage of the arbitrage. Specifically, APs will buy the basket of securities that the ETF tracks (the creation basket) and exchange it with the ETF sponsor for new ETF shares (a creation unit). These new ETF shares received by APs can then be sold on the open market to realize arbitrage profits.

    B is incorrect because in the case of an ETF trading at a premium to NAV, the APs will not receive redemption baskets of securities. Instead, the APs will deliver creation baskets to the ETF sponsor and receive new ETF shares.

    C is incorrect because only APs can deliver creation baskets or receive redemption baskets from the ETF sponsors. Retail investors can buy and sell ETF shares on the open market.

20. A is correct. Compared with a full replication approach, ETF portfolios managed using a representative sampling/optimization approach are likely to have greater tracking error. Also, differences in trading hours for depositary receipts and local constituent shares create discrepancies between the portfolio and index values. These discrepancies can lead to greater tracking error for portfolios holding ADRs in lieu of the underlying local shares. Further, ETF sponsors that engage in securities lending can generate additional portfolio income to help offset fund expenses, thereby lowering tracking error. ETF 2 uses a full replication approach, holds only local foreign shares, and engages in securities lending. Therefore, ETF 2 will likely have the lowest tracking error out of the ETFs in Exhibit 1. ETF 3 will likely have greater tracking error than ETF 2 because it is managed using a representative sampling approach and is invested in depositary receipts in lieu of local shares. ETF 4 will likely have greater tracking error than ETF 2 because it is invested in depositary receipts in lieu of local shares and does not engage in securities lending.

21. C is correct. Several factors determine the width of an ETF's quoted bid–ask spread. First, the amount of ongoing order flow in the ETF is negatively related to the bid–ask spread (more flow means lower spreads). Second, the actual costs and risks for the liquidity provider are positively related to spreads (more costs and risks mean higher spreads); the spread is compensation to the liquidity provider for incurring these costs and risks. Finally, the amount of competition among market makers for that ETF is negatively related to the bid–ask spread (more competition means lower spreads).

    A is incorrect because Stosur is correct in stating that the quoted bid–ask spread for a particular transaction size is negatively related to the amount of the ongoing order flow in the ETF (more flow means lower spreads).

    B is incorrect because Stosur is correct in stating that the quoted bid–ask spread for a particular transaction size is positively related to the costs and risks for the ETF liquidity provider (more costs and risks mean higher spreads). The bid–ask spread represents the market maker's price for taking the other side of the ETF transaction, which includes the costs and risks to carry the position on its books and/or to hedge the position using underlying securities or closely related ETFs or derivatives.

22. C is correct. ETFs that trade infrequently may have large premiums or discounts to NAV, because the ETF may not have traded in the hours leading up to the market close and NAV may have significantly risen or fallen during that time because of market movement. Furthermore, NAV is often a poor fair value indicator for ETFs holding foreign securities because of differences in exchange closing times between the underlying (e.g., foreign stocks, bonds, or commodities) and the exchange where the ETF trades. Therefore, ETF 7 is most likely to have the largest discount or premium because it has a low trading frequency and has the highest percentage of foreign holdings among the three ETFs.

A is incorrect because ETF 5 has the lowest percentage of foreign holdings among the three ETFs and is the one ETF with a high trading frequency. Therefore, relative to ETF 7, with its low trading frequency and high foreign holdings, ETF 5 is likely to trade at smaller premiums or discounts.

B is incorrect because ETF 6 has a lower percentage of foreign holdings than ETF 7. Even though both ETF 6 and ETF 7 have the same low trading frequency, the lower percentage of foreign holdings for ETF 6 is likely to result in it trading at smaller premiums or discounts.

23. A is correct. The expected total holding period cost for investing in the ETF over the nine-month holding period is calculated as follows:

Total expected holding period cost = Annual management fee + Round-trip trading commissions + Bid–offer spread on purchase/sale.

Total expected holding period cost = (9/12) × (0.32%) + 0.20% + 0.10% = 0.54%.

CASE STUDY IN PORTFOLIO MANAGEMENT: INSTITUTIONAL

SOLUTIONS

1. **Identify** which asset classes Bookman is *most likely* to note as in need of rebalancing band policy adjustment. [Circle choice(s)]

   Justify your selection(s).

   Cash
   Fixed Income
   Public Equity

   Private Equity

   Real Assets

   As part of effective portfolio management, rebalancing disciplines, such as calendar rebalancing and percent-range rebalancing, are intended to control risk relative to the strategic asset allocation. In these cases, pre-specified Tolerance bands for asset class weights are used. The size or width of the bands should consider the underlying volatility of each investment category to minimize transaction costs. This means more-volatile investment categories usually have wider rebalancing bands.

   Cash Rebalancing:
   In reply to the university investment committee as it performs its quarterly assessment, Bookman notes that the cash asset classes have the lowest standard deviation with one of the widest rebalancing band policies. The cash rebalancing band should be evaluated and suitably reduced.
   Private Equity Rebalancing: The private equity asset class also has the highest standard deviation with one of the tightest rebalancing band policies. The private equity rebalancing band should be evaluated and suitably expanded.

2. To operationalize the concepts represented in the liquidity budget, it is appropriate to analyze the underlying liquidity characteristics of the portfolio investments and monitor these characteristics over time. The analysis should look beyond the broad definition of asset classes to the underlying investments used for exposure as different investments within the same asset class may have very different liquidity profiles.

In performing a bottom-up liquidity analysis on the State Tech endowment, Bookman multiplies each asset class allocation by its matching liquidity classification and then aggregates across asset classes. Based on this analysis, 44.5% of investments are currently classified as liquid and 28.5% are classified as illiquid, calculated as follows:

Investments classified as liquid = (Cash allocation × %Liquid)
 + (Fixed-income allocation × %Liquid) + (Public equity allocation × %Liquid)

Investments classified as liquid = (1% × 100%) + (24% × 100%)
 + (39% × 50%) = 44.5%.

Investments classified as illiquid = (Private equity allocation × %Illiquid)
 + (Real asset allocation × %Illiquid)

Investments classified as illiquid = (21% × 100%) + (15% × 50%) = 28.5%.

The liquid investment allocation of 44.5% is well above the 30% liquid requirement, and the 28.5% illiquid investment allocation is well below the 40% illiquid limit. As a result, there is enough capacity to re-allocate more funds from liquid investments into illiquid investments to take advantage of the higher potential returns. Thus, Bookman can recommend that shift.

3. **Determine if** Heard's statements are correct.

Statement 1 (Circle one)	Statement 2 (Circle one)
Correct Incorrect	Correct Incorrect
Justify your response.	**Justify** your response.
Statement 1 is incorrect because of a misunderstanding of the characteristics of particular investments. The endowment should shift funds into private equity and real estate as these asset classes generally offer a higher return potential due to higher liquidity premiums. However, within these asset classes the endowment should target longer-term investments, not shorter term. Longer-term investments tend to be the most illiquid and offer the highest liquidity premium. Quantitative estimates for the illiquidity premium suggest evidence of a positive illiquidity premium in private equity and private real estate and of illiquidity premium size being positively correlated to the length of the illiquidity horizon.	Statement 2 is incorrect because of a misinterpretation of the effects of the illiquidity premium. Heard's statement on public equities is partially true, but it does not rely on a fully defensible basis for an investment recommendation. While a significant body of literature documents a positive relationship between lack of liquidity and expected returns in the case of public equity, overall it is difficult to isolate the illiquidity premium with precision and separate its effects from such other risk factors as the market, value, and size in the case of equity investments. Furthermore, estimates of the illiquidity premium are based on broad market indexes, yet an investor in these asset classes would typically invest in only a small subset of the universe with the result that individual investment experience could be very different and more susceptible to idiosyncratic factors. These challenges further emphasize the importance of liquidity budgeting in facilitating capture of the illiquidity premium while controlling for risk.

4. Private equity is recognized as an illiquid alternative investment and may offer higher returns via a liquidity premium.
    The illiquidity premium (also called the liquidity premium) is the expected compensation for the additional risk of tying up capital for a potentially uncertain time period. It can be estimated, as Smith has done, by using the idea that the size of a discount an investor should receive for such capital commitment is represented by the value of a put option with an exercise price equal to the hypothetical "marketable price" of the illiquid asset as estimated at the time of purchase. Smith can derive the price of the illiquid private equity asset by subtracting the put price from the "marketable price." If both the "marketable price" and the illiquid asset price are estimated or known, then the expected return for each can be calculated, with the difference in expected returns representing the illiquidity premium (in %).

5. Reasons to justify the increased risk profile include the following:
    a. The board members' lower return expectations for public equity and fixed-income asset classes imply a higher level of risk must be taken to achieve the same level of returns.
    b. For a long-horizon institutional investor like Pell Tech, the ability to tolerate illiquidity creates an opportunity to improve portfolio diversification and expected returns as well as access a broader set of investment strategies. In mean–variance optimization models, the inclusion of illiquid assets in the eligible investment universe may shift the efficient frontier for their portfolio upwards, theoretically resulting in greater efficiency (i.e., higher expected returns will be gained across all given levels of risk).
    c. The portfolio risk profile for the endowment is currently more conservative in comparison to those of peer universities.
    d. Smith's Monte Carlo simulations suggest that the proposed asset allocation has a higher probability of achieving the return target while better preserving the purchasing power of the endowment.

6. In voicing his concerns, Brodka is cautioning that a higher allocation to illiquid investments may have adverse effects on the endowment's spending rate and risk profile. Kemney University's spending policy is an example of a geometric smoothing rule, sometimes called the Yale formula. It is intended to bring about a predictable pattern of distributions for better planning of resource deployment through its programs across varying conditions, even as extreme as the 2008 global financial crisis.
    While this spending policy would be consistent with an investment objective of achieving long-term returns that support the spending rate while preserving the value of the endowment in real terms over time, the policy design also incorporates a smoothing, countercyclical element. This leads to lower spending rates in a period of sustained strong investment returns but higher spending rates in a protracted weak return environment.

7. As a result of the allocation changes, there will be a reduction in the liquid and semi-liquid categories and an increase in the illiquid category under both normal and stress conditions. The proposed allocation shifting 5% of the endowment's investments from liquid to illiquid assets would result in an increase in the overall illiquidity profile.
    Regarding Brodka's concern about the liquidity profile, Grides needs to ensure that even under stress conditions the proposed allocation continues to comply with the liquidity budgeting framework in place. From an ongoing management perspective—and particularly at times when the liquidity profile of the proposed allocation is closer to the minimum thresholds set through the liquidity budget—Grides should plan to closely

monitor the portfolio's liquidity profile and stress test it periodically to make sure portfolio liquidity remains adequate.

Regarding Brodka's concern of risk profile "drift," illiquid assets carry extremely high rebalancing costs. Because asset liquidity tends to decrease in periods of market stress, it is important to have sufficient liquid assets and rebalancing mechanisms in place to ensure the portfolio's risk profile remains within acceptable risk targets and does not "drift" as the relative valuations of different asset classes fluctuate during stress periods. Since liquid assets will decrease due to the proposed allocation, Grides must ensure an effective rebalancing mechanism is adopted prior to the investment and is consistently followed thereafter. That mechanism can be through a systematic discipline, such as calendar rebalancing or percent-range rebalancing that sets pre-specified tolerance bands for asset weights. Or, an automatic rebalancing method can be adopted, such as by using adjustments to a public market allocation that is correlated to a private market allocation (likely a more illiquid exposure) to rebalance private market risk.

Contrary to its desired intent, and providing grounds for Brodka's concerns, this design would exacerbate the endowment's liquidity needs in severe market downturns. Given the possibility of such adverse events within Kemney's long-term planning horizon, the policy is very relevant as potentially introducing undesired risks.

8. Dixon's actions and conduct pose multiple ethical concerns.

Dixon's claim of compliance statement and cover letter, along with Langhorne's performance report, violate both the CFA Institute Code of Ethics and Standards of Professional Conduct (Code and Standards) and the GIPS standards. Regarding the Code and Standards, Dixon's statement improperly asserts that CFA Institute has designated Langhorne as a "member firm." Membership is held by practitioners as individuals, with no related rights extended to the firms at which they work. With this assertion, Dixon has misrepresented Langhorne's claim of compliance, Standard I(C): Professionalism, Misrepresentation; engaged in conduct that compromised the reputation or integrity of CFA Institute, Standard VII(A): Responsibilities as a CFA Institute Member or CFA Institute Candidate, Conduct as Participants in CFA Institute Programs; and misrepresented or exaggerated the meaning or implications of membership in CFA Institute, Standard VII(B): Responsibilities as a CFA Institute Member or CFA Institute Candidate, Reference to CFA Institute, the CFA Designation, and the CFA Program.

Regarding the GIPS standards and the performance report, presenting composite returns on a net-of-fees basis is acceptable under the GIPS standards. However, it is not appropriate to adjust benchmark returns with a hypothetical fee for comparative purposes (i.e., composite gross-of-fees returns should be compared to unadjusted benchmark returns). This adjustment of Langhorne's performance report is invalid under the GIPS standards under Section 4.a.1: Disclosure—Requirements. The 1.00% hypothetical fee deducted from benchmark returns is surely greater than the average fee deducted in arriving at composite net-of-fees returns. An average portfolio size of $60 million implies a composite fee percentage of roughly 0.63%, or: {(0.0100 × $5 million) + [0.0060 × ($60 million − $5 million)]}/$60 million = 0.0063 or 0.63%. So, on a relative basis, deducting a larger cost against the benchmark will show Langhorne with a phantom outperformance.

In terms of the Code and Standards, at a minimum, Dixon has presented an inaccurate performance comparison—Standard III(D): Duties to Clients, Performance Presentation—

and may have engaged in misrepresentation to the point of misconduct—Standard I(D): Professionalism, Misconduct—since it may be deceitful to cast a more favorable light on the Langhorne composite net-of-fees returns (Section 0.A.7 under Fundamentals of Compliance—Requirements of the GIPS standards).

Dixon's cover letter invitation for an all-expenses paid outing to an exclusive golf destination can be construed as an attempt to influence the independence and objectivity of the Foundation's CIO and president—Standard I(B): Professionalism, Independence and Objectivity. While Dixon's invitation was extended "regardless of the outcome of the manager search," the offer could be interpreted as a *quid pro quo*, with future attractive personal benefits available to the Foundation's executives if a continuing relationship was established by their hiring of Langhorne as a manager.

9. As the lower cost alternative, the endowment's investment team should implement the 1% overweight position using futures.

The additional cost of obtaining leverage for each option is as follows:

ETF: ($5 million × 0.6667 × 2.15%) / $5 million = 1.43% (or 143 bps)

Futures: ($5 million × 0.6667 × 1.80%) / $5 million = 1.20% (or 120 bps)

where the inputs are derived as follows:

0.6667 reflects the 3 times leverage factor (66.67% borrowed and 33.33% cash usage)

2.15% reflects the ETF borrowing rate (3-month Libor of 1.80% + 35 bps)

1.80% reflects the absence of investment income offset (at 3-month Libor) versus the
unlevered cost of futures implementation

The total levered cost of each option is the sum of the unlevered cost plus the additional cost of obtaining leverage:

ETF: 27 bps + 143 bps = 170 bps

Futures: 32 bps + 120 bps = 152 bps

This 18 bps cost advantage would make futures the appropriate choice for the endowment's investment team.

---

10. **Compare** the efficiency of the ETF and total return swap TAA implementation alternatives from the perspectives of capital commitment, liquidity, and tracking error.

Capital Commitment:
From a cash "usage" perspective, a Russell 1000 Growth ETF would be less efficient (requiring a larger cash outlay) than a total return swap replicating the Russell 1000 Growth Index. The capital commitment of an unlevered ETF equals the full notional value. In contrast, a total return swap generates a similar economic exposure to ETFs with much lower capital. The cash-efficient nature of derivatives, such as total return swaps, makes them desirable tools for gaining incremental exposure to a particular asset class.

Liquidity:
From a liquidity perspective, a Russell 1000 Growth ETF would be more efficient than the total return swap. As exchange-traded standardized products, ETFs enjoy liquid trading and narrow bid–ask spreads. In contrast, total return swaps are over-the-counter contracts (not exchange traded) that are negotiated and customizable on such features as maturity, leverage, and cost.

Tracking Error:
From a tracking error perspective, ETFs would be less efficient than the total return swap. A Russell 1000 Growth ETF would have associated tracking error, which may result from premiums and discounts to net asset value, cash drag, or regulatory diversification requirements. In contrast, for total return swaps, the replication is exact. The Foundation would receive the total index return without incurring any tracking error to the benchmark index because the swap counterparty is obligated to provide the index return. This would, however, expose the Foundation to counterparty credit risk and introduce additional complexities in managing net exposure over the duration of the contract.

---

11. **Determine** the *most appropriate* rebalancing choice for the Foundation's investment team. (Circle one)

| Cash Market | Derivatives Market |

Justify your response.

The Foundation's investment team should execute the rebalancing in the derivatives market rather than the cash market. The team could, for example, establish a 1.2% long position to the S&P 500 Index using short-term S&P 500 futures to rebalance the US public equities asset class back to its policy allocation corridor.
Execution in the derivatives market offers the following advantages:
• Quick implementation
• Flexibility to tactically adjust exposure and quickly reverse decisions
• Ability to leave external managers in place
• High levels of liquidity
The team views the sell-off as temporary and is pleased with external manager performance. This suggests a short-term rebalancing approach is warranted rather than reallocating among managers. Execution in the derivatives market will enable quick rebalancing while leaving current allocations in place.
The sell-off has increased the significance of liquidity and flexibility. The derivatives market offers flexibility to quickly adjust market exposures with high levels of liquidity.
While derivatives can present tracking error and operational risks, the expected short-term nature of the rebalancing serves to contain their effects. The benefits to be gained using derivatives appear to more than outweigh the associated cost and risk.

CFA Institute

ABOUT THE
CFA PROGRAM

If the subject matter of this book interests you, and you are not already a CFA Charterholder, we hope you will consider registering for the CFA Program and starting progress toward earning the Chartered Financial Analyst designation. The CFA designation is a globally recognized standard of excellence for measuring the competence and integrity of investment professionals. To earn the CFA charter, candidates must successfully complete the CFA Program, a global graduate-level self-study program that combines a broad curriculum with professional conduct requirements as preparation for a career as an investment professional.

Anchored in a practice-based curriculum, the CFA Program body of knowledge reflects the knowledge, skills, and abilities identified by professionals as essential to the investment decision-making process. This body of knowledge maintains its relevance through a regular, extensive survey of practicing CFA charterholders across the globe. The curriculum covers 10 general topic areas, ranging from equity and fixed-income analysis to portfolio management to corporate finance—all with a heavy emphasis on the application of ethics in professional practice. Known for its rigor and breadth, the CFA Program curriculum highlights principles common to every market so that professionals who earn the CFA designation have a thoroughly global investment perspective and a profound understanding of the global marketplace.

www.cfainstitute.org